SAMARA ZEN

Mindful Living: Transform Your Life with the Power of Meditation

Contents

Introduction

Welcome to a journey that promises to enhance your mental well-being, reduce stress, and bring a greater sense of peace and self-awareness into your life. The practice of mindfulness and meditation serves as an anchor in today's fast-paced world, offering a respite from the constant barrage of information and endless to-do lists. This book aims to provide you not merely with knowledge but with actionable steps to integrate these practices into your daily routine.

In recent years, the conversation around mental health has broadened, acknowledging that well-being isn't just the absence of illness; it's a holistic state of thriving, both mentally and physically. Mindfulness and meditation come to the forefront as vital tools in achieving this balanced state. These practices aren't new. They're rooted in ancient traditions, honed over millennia, yet they hold remarkable relevance in our modern lives.

Think about the moments when you're overwhelmed, your mind racing from one task to the next, and stress seems insurmountable. Now imagine a genuine, reliable way to manage these feelings, allowing you to face every challenge with a sense of calm and clarity. This isn't a far-fetched dream. It's possible with mindfulness and meditation. These aren't magical cures, but they are powerful tools in a comprehensive mental health toolkit, enabling profound changes if used consistently.

In this book, you'll find a structured approach to understanding, adopting, and mastering these practices. Each chapter is designed to build upon the previous one, guiding you from a basic understanding of mindfulness to its application in complex, real-world scenarios. We'll dive into the science behind mindfulness, unveiling why and how these techniques work.

Whether you're a complete beginner who's just heard the term "mindfulness," or someone looking to deepen an existing practice, this book offers value. We'll start from the basics—understanding what mindfulness is and where it comes from. From there, we'll explore the numerous benefits of meditation, offering compelling reasons to make it a daily habit.

Creating new habits isn't easy, and the journey to mindfulness can sometimes feel overwhelming. That's why it's important to set yourself up for success right from the start. We'll discuss how to create a conducive environment for practice, choose techniques that resonate with you, and integrate mindfulness into daily life—turning ordinary actions like eating or walking into mindful experiences.

Challenges are a part of any journey, and the path to mindfulness is no exception. Be it distractions, self-doubt, or finding the time, we'll share strategies to overcome these hurdles. You'll also find guided meditations designed specifically for beginners. If you're new to this, you'll appreciate the gentle, step-by-step approach that makes these techniques accessible and easy to follow.

As you progress, you'll learn how to deepen your practice, extending meditation times and exploring advanced techniques to keep you engaged and motivated. The benefits of mindfulness go beyond individual well-being; they'll spill over into your relationships and professional life, enhancing how you connect with others and perform at work.

Incorporating mindfulness into your daily routine can significantly reduce stress, improve focus, and help manage emotions more effectively. By recognizing emotional triggers and responding mindfully, you can cultivate a sense of peace even in the most challenging circumstances. And who wouldn't want better sleep? We will introduce bedtime routines that incorporate mindfulness for a more restful, rejuvenating sleep experience.

Mindfulness isn't just for adults. If you've got a family, mindfulness can become a beautiful practice shared among all members, including children. Simple techniques tailored for kids make it easy to introduce them to the benefits of mindfulness early on.

In our technologically driven world, balancing mindfulness with constant digital engagement poses unique challenges. But it's completely possible to use technology to our advantage without letting it dominate our lives. This book will provide you with a detailed guide on leveraging digital tools for mindfulness while ensuring you don't fall into the trap of digital overload.

Your mindfulness journey doesn't end here. We'll explore how to sustain your practice over the long term, set realistic goals, and measure your progress. Nature and mindfulness also go hand in hand, and we'll show you how outdoor meditative practices can add a refreshing dimension to your routine.

Many find a spiritual dimension in their mindfulness practice, while others appreciate it purely for its practical benefits. Whichever path you choose, the practice can seamlessly integrate into your personal belief system, making it a truly unique journey for each individual.

The latter chapters of this book bring together stories of transformation and expert testimonials that exemplify the profound impact mindfulness can have. We'll also delve into how these practices have been adopted and adapted across different cultures and countries, providing a global perspective on mindfulness.

The journey ends with a look into the future of mindfulness. Emerging research continues to validate and expand the applications of these ancient practices, offering new insights and methods to enrich our lives. As you turn the last page, our hope is you'll walk away with not just knowledge, but a deeper appreciation and a lifelong practice that brings you closer to peace, focus, and holistic well-being.

So, step into this journey with an open heart and mind, and prepare to transform your life through the simple yet profound power of mindfulness and meditation. Let's embark on this path to mental wellness together.

Chapter 1: Understanding Mindfulness

Mindfulness is more than just a buzzword; it's a state of being fully present and engaged in the moment without judgment. By anchoring ourselves in the present, we can break free from the autopilot mode that often governs our daily lives. It's about noticing the world around us, our thoughts, and our feelings without getting caught up in them. Imagine the mental clarity and peace that comes from truly experiencing each moment as it is, not as we wish it to be. This foundation of mindfulness can transform how we handle stress, stay focused, and connect with ourselves and others. It's the gentle art of paying attention, and mastering it can significantly enhance your mental well-being, leading to a more centered and fulfilling life.

The Science Behind Mindfulness

In recent years, mindfulness has gained significant attention from both practitioners and scientists alike. But what exactly is happening in our brains and bodies when we practice mindfulness? To understand this, it's essential to dive into the science behind it, which reveals that our mental and physical states are deeply intertwined, influencing each other in profound ways.

Research has shown that mindfulness practices can lead to changes in brain structure and function. One of the most remarkable findings is the impact on the brain's gray matter. Studies using MRI scans have indicated that regular mindfulness practice can increase gray matter density in areas of the brain associated with learning, memory, emotion regulation, and empathy. Essentially, practicing mindfulness can physically reshape your brain, enhancing your cognitive and emotional capabilities.

Another key discovery relates to the brain's default mode network (DMN). The DMN is active when our minds are at rest and not focused on the outside world, often leading to mind-wandering and self-referential thoughts. Excessive activity in the DMN is linked to ruminative thinking and depression. Mindfulness has been shown to reduce activity in the DMN, promoting a state of present-moment awareness and reducing the tendency for our minds to drift into negative thought patterns.

From a neurological perspective, mindfulness practice engages several key brain regions. For instance, the prefrontal cortex, responsible for planning, problem-solving, and emotional regulation, shows increased activation. Simultaneously, there's decreased activity in the amygdala, the brain's fear center. This shift helps explain why mindfulness can reduce anxiety and stress, making us more resilient to life's challenges.

Ever noticed how stress seems to affect your entire body? That's because the mind and body are inextricably linked through the nervous system. Mindfulness has a profound impact on the autonomic nervous system, particularly the balance between the sympathetic and parasympathetic branches. The sympathetic nervous system triggers the "fight or flight" response, while the parasympathetic nervous system promotes relaxation and recovery. Regular mindfulness practice can help shift the balance towards parasympathetic activation, promoting a state of calm and reducing overall stress levels.

Moreover, cortisol, often referred to as the stress hormone, is affected by mindfulness practice. Chronic stress keeps cortisol levels elevated, leading to a host of health problems, including weakened immune function and increased inflammation. Mindfulness techniques have been found to lower cortisol levels, helping to mitigate these detrimental effects and contributing to better overall health.

It's not just the brain and stress response that benefit from mindfulness; our immune systems also get a significant boost. Studies have shown that mindfulness practices can increase the activity of natural killer cells, which are vital in the body's defense against infections and cancer. This enhanced immune function supports a more robust and resilient body, equipped to fight off illnesses more effectively.

The science behind mindfulness extends to its impact on genetic expression. Yes, you read that right—mindfulness can influence your genes. Research in the field of epigenetics has shown that mindfulness practices can lead to changes in gene expression, particularly those related to inflammation and stress response. These changes suggest that mindfulness can have long-term, beneficial effects on our health at a molecular level.

When we talk about the science of mindfulness, we can't overlook the role of neurotransmitters. These chemical messengers play a crucial role in transmitting signals across the brain, influencing how we think, feel, and behave. Mindfulness practices have been found to increase the levels of serotonin and dopamine, neurotransmitters associated with happiness and pleasure. Increased levels of these "feel-good" chemicals can contribute to improved mood and overall mental well-being.

It's fascinating how mindfulness can also affect heart health. Research has demonstrated that mindfulness practices can lower blood pressure, a critical factor in cardiovascular health. By reducing stress and promoting relaxation, mindfulness helps to keep your heart and circulatory system functioning optimally, reducing the risk of heart disease and related conditions.

Beyond these physiological benefits, the science of mindfulness encompasses improvements in cognitive functions such as attention and focus. Mindfulness practices train the brain to stay present, enhancing our ability to concentrate and be less distracted. This improvement in attention can translate to better performance in various aspects of life, from work to personal relationships.

One of the most intriguing areas of research is the effect of mindfulness on emotional intelligence. Emotional intelligence involves understanding and managing our own emotions as well as empathizing with others. Studies have shown that mindfulness practices can enhance these skills, making us more adept at navigating social interactions and forming healthier, more fulfilling relationships.

The scientific community has also explored the impact of mindfulness on pain perception. Chronic pain affects millions, and traditional treatments don't always provide relief. Mindfulness practices have been found to alter the perception of pain, helping individuals manage chronic pain more effectively by changing their relationship with the discomfort and reducing the emotional and psychological distress associated with it.

Furthermore, mindfulness can play a critical role in addiction recovery. The practice can help individuals become more aware of their cravings and triggers, allowing them to respond in a more measured and controlled way. By fostering a greater sense of self-awareness and emotional regulation, mindfulness can be a powerful tool in overcoming addictive behaviors.

The science behind mindfulness is continually evolving, with new studies and findings emerging regularly. These discoveries not only affirm the benefits that many practitioners have experienced but also provide a deeper understanding of the mechanisms at play. As our knowledge grows, the potential for applying mindfulness in various fields—from education to healthcare—becomes even more exciting and promising.

Ultimately, the scientific backing for mindfulness underscores its efficacy and broadens its appeal. Whether you're just starting your mindfulness journey or have been practicing for years, understanding the science behind it can provide motivation and insight, enriching your practice and reinforcing the many ways mindfulness can contribute to a healthier, happier life.

Historical Roots

When we talk about mindfulness, it's easy to think it's a modern concept, conjured up by stressed-out urbanites searching for peace amidst the chaos. However, its roots stretch back thousands of years, much deeper than any current self-help fad. To truly appreciate the benefits and the scope of mindfulness practice, it's essential to understand where it came from.

The foundations of mindfulness are deeply embedded in ancient Eastern traditions, particularly within the spiritual practices of Buddhism. Siddhartha Gautama, better known as Buddha, is often credited with formalizing methods resembling contemporary mindfulness around the 5th century BCE. Through his teachings, mindfulness was framed as a path to enlightenment, a means to alleviate suffering and achieve a state of profound understanding and inner peace.

Mindfulness in the context of Buddhism is referred to as "sati" in Pali and "smṛti" in Sanskrit. These terms encapsulate the concepts of awareness, attention, and remembering. For the Buddhists, mindfulness wasn't just a practice, but a way of perceiving and interacting with the world. It's about cultivating an ongoing, heightened state of awareness.

Yet, mindfulness isn't exclusive to Buddhism. Hinduism, too, incorporates mindfulness within its practices. In Hindu texts like the Bhagavad Gita and the Upanishads, there are numerous references to meditative practices aimed at focusing the mind and achieving spiritual insight. These practices often involve concentrating on the breath, chanting, and visualization techniques.

While Buddhism and Hinduism played significant roles in the development of mindfulness, it's fascinating to note that elements of mindfulness practice can be found in many of the world's spiritual traditions. In Christianity, the practice of contemplative prayer shares similarities with mindfulness meditation—focusing the mind and seeking a deeper connection with the divine. Sufism, a mystical branch of Islam, employs practices like breathing exercises and dance to achieve a higher state of spiritual awareness, aligning closely with the principles of mindfulness.

As we journey through history, we begin to see how mindfulness wasn't confined to the East. In the Stoic philosophy of ancient Greece, mindfulness principles were evident. Philosophers like Epictetus and Marcus Aurelius wrote extensively about the importance of living in the present moment and maintaining a disciplined, focused mind. Their writings reflect an understanding that mindfulness is not purely about meditation but living thoughtfully and with intention.

Fast forward to the 20th century, and we observe that mindfulness gracefully leapt across cultural boundaries, gaining recognition in the West. This shift was significantly influenced by a blend of Eastern wisdom and Western psychology. Pioneers like Jon Kabat-Zinn played a crucial role.

Kabat-Zinn, a professor of medicine, founded the Mindfulness-Based Stress Reduction (MBSR) program in the late 1970s, integrating Buddhist principles of mindfulness with scientific practices. His work marked a turning point, illuminating how mindfulness could be secular, accessible, and impactful for anyone seeking mental clarity and peace.

The integration of mindfulness into Western medicine and psychology brought about rigorous scientific research, validating what ancient practitioners knew all along: mindfulness works. It's this blend of ancient wisdom and modern science that has made mindfulness such a powerful tool for enhancing mental well-being.

While figures like Kabat-Zinn helped make mindfulness mainstream, they stood on centuries of tradition and teachings. Understanding this lineage enriches our appreciation and practice, knowing that each moment of mindfulness connects us to a vast, interconnected past. What we practice today is the culmination of countless lifetimes of searching, experimenting, and refining ways to understand the mind and relieve suffering.

The journey of mindfulness from ancient temples and monasteries to modern-day living rooms, classrooms, and therapy sessions speaks volumes about its universality and effectiveness. It's an enduring testament to our shared human quest for peace, understanding, and connection. By integrating the historical and philosophical roots of mindfulness, we can practice with a richer perspective, honoring the generations before us who paved the way.

So, when you sit down to your practice, remember that you're not just part of a contemporary wellness trend. You're engaging in a deeply historical, spiritual, and human experience. You're tapping into a legacy of wisdom that's transcended time, culture, and geography—all in your pursuit of a more mindful, serene life.

This connection to the past can be incredibly motivating. It reminds us that mindfulness isn't about achieving perfection or an elevated state of being. Instead, it's about being present, open, and connected to the world and to ourselves. The historical roots of mindfulness highlight that this journey has been ventured by many before us, and we, too, can navigate it with grace and intention.

In summary, the historical roots of mindfulness are a mosaic of diverse traditions and practices, all converging on a single point: the human desire for a peaceful mind and a fulfilled life. From sages and philosophers of antiquity to modern practitioners and scientists, the essence of mindfulness remains timeless. It's a continuous thread woven through the fabric of human existence, guiding us towards understanding and peace. And as we adopt it in our lives, we contribute to its enduring legacy, embodying a practice that is as ancient as it is profoundly relevant today.

Chapter 2: The Benefits of Meditation

The benefits of meditation are vast and transformative, touching nearly every aspect of our lives. It enhances physical health by lowering blood pressure, improving sleep quality, and boosting the immune system. On the mental front, meditation reduces stress and anxiety, sharpens focus, and promotes a profound sense of inner peace. Imagine starting your day with a clear mind and a calm heart, ready to face any challenge that comes your way. Meditation also fosters self-awareness, helping you to understand your emotions and reactions better, which can lead to healthier relationships and a more balanced life. By committing to a regular meditation practice, you're not just enhancing your mental well-being; you're paving the way for a more mindful, enriched, and harmonious existence.

Physical Health Benefits

Meditation does far more than just calm the mind; it also has a significant impact on physical health. Through various practices, the body can reap profound benefits that boost well-being and resilience. These physical health benefits are vast and affect many aspects of our bodily functions, from the heart to the immune system. Let's delve into some of the most impactful ways your body benefits from a regular meditation practice.

One of the most well-documented benefits of meditation is its ability to reduce stress. Chronic stress can wreak havoc on the body, leading to a host of issues like high blood pressure, heart disease, and digestive problems. When we meditate, we get a chance to reset and calm the nervous system. This process reduces the production of stress hormones like cortisol. Lower levels of cortisol mean less strain on the heart and a decrease in inflammation, which can lead to fewer stress-related ailments.

Regular meditation can also significantly improve cardiovascular health. Studies have shown that individuals who meditate consistently have lower blood pressure compared to those who don't. The practice helps to relax the blood vessels, improving blood flow and reducing the workload on the heart. This can be particularly beneficial for those at risk of hypertension or other cardiovascular diseases. Over time, better cardiovascular health leads to increased longevity and a better quality of life.

Apart from its cardiovascular benefits, meditation also strengthens the immune system. Your body is better equipped to fight off illnesses when you're less stressed and more relaxed. Stress can weaken the immune response, making you more susceptible to colds, infections, and even more severe diseases. Meditation helps to mitigate this by enhancing the body's ability to respond to threats effectively. This makes it easier to maintain good health and recover quickly if you do fall ill.

An often overlooked benefit of meditation is its influence on sleep. Poor sleep can lead to a myriad of health problems, including obesity, diabetes, and immune dysfunction. Meditation encourages a state of relaxation that makes it easier to fall asleep and stay asleep. Techniques such as focused breathing and body scanning can help to quiet the mind and release physical tension, setting the stage for restful slumber. Over time, better sleep can drastically improve overall health and vitality.

Another fascinating area where meditation has shown promise is in managing chronic pain. Conditions like arthritis, fibromyalgia, and lower back pain can be debilitating and affect the quality of life. While it may seem counterintuitive, focusing attention on the pain can actually help reduce its intensity. Pain is not just a physical sensation but also an emotional experience. By using mindfulness techniques to observe the pain without getting wrapped up in it, sufferers can diminish their perception of pain and improve their ability to cope.

Meditation also promotes better gastrointestinal health. The gut-brain connection is a hot topic in modern science, and stress plays a huge role in digestive health. Practices that promote relaxation can also help to regulate digestion, alleviating issues such as irritable bowel syndrome (IBS) and acid reflux. By calming the mind and body, the digestive system can function more efficiently, reducing bloating, pain, and other uncomfortable symptoms.

Moreover, meditation supports respiratory health. Deep breathing techniques used in certain forms of meditation can increase lung capacity and improve oxygenation of the blood. This can be particularly beneficial for those with respiratory issues like asthma or chronic obstructive pulmonary disease (COPD). Improved respiratory function not only enhances physical health but also supports mental clarity and energy levels.

In addition to these benefits, meditation can also enhance physical fitness. While often viewed as a mental exercise, the practice helps the body by improving focus, balance, and coordination. This can be particularly beneficial for athletes or anyone looking to enhance their physical performance. The increased awareness of the body and its movements can lead to more effective and safer workouts, reducing the risk of injury.

We can't ignore the fact that meditation also encourages overall lifestyle changes that contribute to physical health. As mindfulness grows, you're more likely to make healthier choices regarding diet, exercise, and sleep. This integrated approach to well-being creates a positive feedback loop, where physical health supports mental well-being and vice versa. Over time, these small changes add up, leading to significant improvements in your quality of life.

Furthermore, the practice can be particularly useful during recovery from surgery or illness. Meditation can speed up recovery times by reducing stress, enhancing immune function, and improving sleep. Patients who meditate often report feeling less anxious and more in control during their recovery periods. This emotional resilience translates into physical resilience, aiding in faster, more comprehensive recovery.

Lastly, it's essential to highlight how meditation reduces inflammation throughout the body. Chronic inflammation is linked to numerous health issues, including autoimmune diseases, cancer, and Alzheimer's disease. The calming effects of meditation can help reduce pro-inflammatory cytokines, the body's signaling molecules that trigger inflammation. By keeping inflammation in check, meditation contributes to a healthier, more balanced internal environment.

In conclusion, the physical health benefits of meditation are both profound and far-reaching. From enhancing cardiovascular health to improving immune function, reducing inflammation, and aiding in pain management, meditation acts as a holistic tool for physical well-being. By incorporating regular meditation into your routine, you can transform not just your mental state, but also your body's health, leading to a more vibrant, energetic, and balanced life.

Mental Health Benefits

Meditation isn't just about finding a few moments of peace in your busy day. It's a powerful practice that offers substantial mental health benefits that can transform your overall well-being. For anyone seeking to reduce stress, improve focus, and achieve a greater sense of peace and self-awareness, the practice of meditation holds immense promise.

One of the most profound mental health benefits of meditation is its impact on stress reduction. Stress is an all-too-common companion in our modern lives, contributing to a range of physical and mental health issues. Through meditation, we can develop the skill of mindfulness—learning to observe our thoughts and emotions without judgement. This mindful approach allows us to manage our reactions to stressors more effectively, reducing the intensity and duration of stress responses. It's like building a buffer between you and the pressures of daily life.

Beyond stress relief, meditation has been shown to alleviate symptoms of anxiety and depression. By fostering a state of mental clarity and emotional stability, meditation helps you gain perspective on the challenges you face. When practiced consistently, it can lead to changes in brain structure and function, particularly in areas related to anxiety and depression. It's as if meditation tunes the brain into a calmer, more reasoned frequency, helping counteract the negative thought patterns that fuel these conditions.

Another significant benefit of meditation is its ability to improve focus and concentration. In a world where we're constantly bombarded with information and distractions, maintaining focus can be incredibly challenging. Meditation trains the mind to return to the present moment, even when it drifts away. Over time, this practice can enhance your ability to concentrate on tasks, improving productivity and efficiency in all areas of life. Think of it as sharpening the mind's focus lens, allowing clearer, more directed attention.

In addition to improving focus, meditation encourages emotional health by fostering a deeper connection with oneself. This self-awareness allows for a greater understanding of personal needs, values, and desires. Through meditation, you cultivate a compassionate inner dialogue, replacing self-criticism with kindness. This shift in self-perception can lead to higher self-esteem and a more resilient mindset, essential for navigating life's ups and downs.

Emotional regulation is another critical mental health benefit of meditation. The practice encourages a balanced emotional state, helping individuals respond to situations with calm and clarity rather than impulsive reactions. Through mindfulness, you become more attuned to your emotions without becoming overwhelmed by them. This equanimity is particularly beneficial when dealing with anger, frustration, or sadness, as it allows for a measured response rather than an immediate upheaval.

Meditation also holds promise for enhancing social connections. When you practice mindfulness, you develop greater empathy and compassion for others. By being present in the moment and truly listening during interactions, your relationships can become more meaningful and fulfilling. This enhanced connectivity not only enriches your social life but can also offer a robust support system, crucial for mental well-being.

On a cognitive level, meditation has been linked to improvements in memory and cognitive function. Regular meditation practice can increase gray matter density in the brain, particularly in regions associated with memory, learning, and self-awareness. As a result, meditation practitioners often experience better recall and greater cognitive flexibility. By maintaining a regular meditation routine, you may find that your mental acuity sharpens, allowing you to navigate daily tasks and challenges with greater ease.

Lastly, meditation can be a powerful tool in combatting addictive behaviors. Whether it's smoking, drinking, or overeating, habits formed as coping mechanisms can be difficult to break. Meditation aids in developing the self-awareness needed to recognize these patterns and offers a meditative pause before impulsively acting on cravings. By fostering a non-judgmental awareness of these urges, meditation provides the mental space needed to choose healthier actions.

It's essential to remember that the benefits of meditation are cumulative— it takes time and consistent practice to reap the full rewards. Starting with just a few minutes a day can set you on a path to significant mental health improvements. Over time, this practice can become a cornerstone of your daily routine, offering lasting peace and mental resilience.

So, as you consider integrating meditation into your life, think about the myriad ways it can enhance your mental health. From reducing stress and anxiety to improving focus, emotional regulation, and social connections, the benefits are both profound and far-reaching. Begin your journey with small, manageable steps, and watch as the transformative power of meditation unfolds in your life. You've got the tools, now it's time to use them.

Chapter 3: Starting Your Meditation Practice

Beginning your meditation journey can feel like stepping into a new world, but with the right preparation, it becomes a transformative experience. Start by setting up a dedicated meditation space—a quiet corner with minimal distractions where you can comfortably sit or lie down. The next step is choosing the technique that resonates with you; whether it's focusing on your breath, repeating a mantra, or visualizing a peaceful scene, finding the right fit will make all the difference. Remember, there's no one-size-fits-all approach here. It's about discovering what helps you tap into a state of calm and clarity. As you begin, give yourself some grace and patience; progress in meditation, much like life, isn't always linear. Just commit to showing up, even for a few minutes each day, and you'll soon start to notice the profound benefits it brings to your mind and spirit.

Setting Up a Meditation Space

Creating a dedicated meditation space can set the stage for a practice that's not only effective but also deeply enjoyable. While having a specific spot to meditate isn't a strict necessity, it can really help foster a sense of commitment and consistency. Think of it as creating a sanctuary where you can disconnect from the daily hustle and reconnect with yourself.

The first thing to consider is where this space should be. Ideally, it should be a quiet, comfortable corner of your home where you're unlikely to be interrupted. It doesn't need to be a whole room; even a small area will do. The main thing is that it's a place you can associate exclusively with meditation. When you enter this space, your mind and body will begin to recognize that it's time to relax and focus inward.

Once you've identified your spot, think about how you can make it comfortable. A soft cushion or a meditation bench can be great, especially if you'll be sitting for longer periods. The aim is to find a seat that allows you to sit upright with ease, providing enough comfort to keep you from fidgeting but not so much that you'll fall asleep. Some people prefer to meditate on a chair, which is perfectly fine as long as you can keep your back straight and feet flat on the floor.

Next, consider the ambiance. The surrounding environment plays a critical role in setting the mood. Soft lighting can be more inviting and less harsh on the eyes than bright overhead lights. You might use candles or a small lamp with a warm light. Adding elements like a small indoor plant can also bring a sense of nature and tranquility into your space.

Scent can be another powerful tool. Essential oils, incense, or even a room spray with calming fragrances like lavender, sandalwood, or chamomile can enhance your meditation experience. Just make sure that whatever you choose doesn't become a distraction. The key here is subtlety—an overpowering scent can be as disruptive as a loud noise.

Speaking of distractions, aim to minimize the amount of clutter in your meditation space. Clutter can be visually and mentally overwhelming, making it harder to settle into your practice. Try to keep your area tidy and free from unnecessary items. It's about creating a sense of openness and simplicity.

Sound is another element worth pondering. While total silence is ideal for some, others might find it unsettling. Consider gentle background music, nature sounds, or white noise if it helps you concentrate. There are plenty of apps and online resources that offer soundscapes designed to promote relaxation and mindfulness.

Personal touches can also make a big difference. Maybe it's a photo that brings you peace, a meaningful statue, or an inspiring piece of art. These small items can make the space feel uniquely yours, infusing it with positive energy and motivation. However, remember not to overdo it—too many personal items can turn your sanctuary into another source of distraction.

Integration of various sensory elements—touch, sight, sound, smell—can create a comprehensive sensory experience that enriches your meditation practice. You could even include objects that encourage mindful touch, such as a worry stone or a piece of soft fabric. These can offer something tangible to help ground you during your sessions.

If you live with others, setting boundaries around your meditation space might be necessary. Letting household members know that you'll be meditating at a certain time each day can help avoid unexpected interruptions. This not only respects your practice but can also inspire others to consider their own mindfulness routines.

For those who don't have the luxury of setting up a permanent space, a portable setup can work wonders. A mat that can be easily rolled up, a lightweight cushion, or even a folding chair can be transported to a quiet spot whenever you need it. The point is flexibility—you create a space when and where you can.

Lighting can also play a big role in setting the mood for meditation. Natural light is wonderful and can make the space feel more serene. But if natural light isn't an option, consider using a table lamp with a dimmer switch. This allows you to adjust the brightness to your preference, creating either a softly-lit ambiance or a darker, more womb-like space, depending on your mood.

Finally, be mindful of temperature. It's much harder to focus on your breathing and your thoughts when you're too cold or too hot. Layers can be your friend here. Keeping a blanket or shawl nearby to wrap up in during colder months, or having a fan for a gentle breeze in the summer, can make a significant difference.

Setting up a meditation space is a deeply personal process, one that involves listening to your own needs and preferences. It's not about creating a perfect or elaborate sanctuary but finding what makes the space feel right for you. The ultimate goal is to create an environment that supports and enhances your practice, making it easier to cultivate mindfulness and achieve a sense of inner peace. Your meditation space, in essence, should be a physical manifestation of the tranquility you are seeking to bring into your mind and life.

Choosing the Right Technique

Embarking on your meditation journey can feel like entering a vast and unfamiliar landscape. The sheer number of techniques available might overwhelm you at first, but fear not. The key to making this journey fruitful and enjoyable is choosing a meditation technique that resonates with you personally. Let's break down the essential considerations so you can make an informed choice.

You may be wondering, "With so many styles out there, how do I choose the right one?" The answer lies in understanding your own needs and preferences. Different techniques serve different purposes. For instance, if you're looking to manage stress, mindfulness or relaxation meditation might be just what you need. On the other hand, if you're seeking to deepen your focus and concentration, you might lean towards practices like Transcendental Meditation (TM) or Zen meditation.

One of the first things to consider is your own temperament. Are you someone who's naturally inclined towards silence and stillness? If so, you might find seated meditation techniques such as Vipassana or Zazen particularly rewarding. These methods emphasize observing your breath and thoughts without judgment, allowing you to cultivate deep inner calm.

Conversely, if you find it challenging to sit still for extended periods, don't be disheartened. Meditation is not one-size-fits-all, and there are dynamic forms of practice designed specifically for people who need more movement. Techniques like walking meditation or Tai Chi incorporate gentle physical activity, making them perfect for individuals who prefer staying active.

Your lifestyle and daily schedule also play a critical role in determining the best technique for you. If you have a packed schedule with little time to spare, a shorter practice like mindfulness meditation, which can be performed in as little as 5-10 minutes, may be suitable. Alternatively, if you have more time for a structured practice, you could explore techniques that require longer sessions, like some forms of guided meditation or Kriya Yoga.

Another critical factor is your current emotional state. Some forms of meditation are oriented towards fostering emotional balance and healing. Loving-kindness meditation, for instance, focuses on cultivating compassion and empathy, which can be particularly beneficial if you're dealing with feelings of anger, resentment, or grief. Think of it as a way to soften the heart and nurture emotional well-being.

With this in mind, it's crucial to experiment. Don't hesitate to try different techniques to see which resonates most with you. Meditation is a deeply personal practice, and what works for one person might not work for another. It's perfectly okay to start with one method and transition to another as your practice evolves. The goal is to find a technique that you look forward to and that adds value to your life.

You might ask, "Can I combine techniques?" Absolutely. In fact, many practitioners find that a hybrid approach works best for them. For example, you could start with a few minutes of breath awareness to settle the mind, followed by a body scan to release tension, and conclude with a loving-kindness meditation. This variety can keep your practice fresh and prevent it from becoming monotonous.

It can also be beneficial to seek guidance from experienced practitioners or teachers. Their insights can help you navigate the initial learning curve and provide valuable feedback. Joining a meditation group or community can also offer a sense of belonging and support, making your practice more sustainable.

Don't underestimate the power of technology in helping you choose and stick with a technique. There are numerous apps and online platforms offering guided meditations in various styles. These resources can be an excellent starting point, especially if you're uncertain about where to begin.

Ultimately, the best technique is the one you will practice regularly. Consistency is far more important than the specific style you choose. So, pick a technique that feels right for you and fits seamlessly into your life. Remember, meditation is a journey of self-discovery. Allow yourself the freedom to explore and adapt as you grow.

In summary, choosing the right meditation technique requires a bit of self-reflection and experimentation. Consider your temperament, lifestyle, emotional state, and the goals you wish to achieve. Don't be afraid to try different methods and combine them if needed. Seek guidance from experienced practitioners and utilize technological tools to assist you. Most importantly, prioritize consistency over perfection in your practice. With these tips in mind, you're well on your way to finding a technique that will not only enhance your meditation practice but also contribute to your overall sense of well-being.

As you continue your journey, remember that each step you take toward finding the right technique brings you closer to a more peaceful and centered version of yourself. Embrace the process, and trust that you will find what works best for you. Your meditation practice is a gift to yourself—one that will keep giving back in countless ways.

Now that you have a clearer understanding of how to choose the right technique, let's move on to incorporating mindfulness into your daily life. This next chapter will guide you on how to bring the benefits of your meditation practice into every aspect of your day, from eating to walking and beyond.

Chapter 4: Mindfulness in Daily Life

Incorporating mindfulness into your daily routine doesn't have to be a daunting task; it can be as simple and natural as breathing. Imagine transforming everyday activities—like eating a meal or taking a walk—into opportunities to cultivate greater awareness and presence. By intentionally tuning into these moments, you begin to truly experience life, rather than just getting through it on autopilot. This practice allows you to savor the richness of each experience, creating a deeper connection with yourself and your surroundings. It's about finding joy in the mundane and beauty in the routine, making each day a tapestry woven with moments of deliberate attention. You don't need to carve out extra time or space; instead, learn to infuse mindfulness into the spaces already present in your life. When you do, you'll find that the quality of your living improves, stress diminishes, and a profound sense of peace takes root within you.

Mindful Eating

Imagine the last time you ate a meal without distraction. No phone, no TV, no book, just you and your plate. In today's fast-paced world, eating can often become a secondary activity, something we do while multitasking. But what if we could transform eating into a deeply nourishing experience by incorporating mindfulness?

Mindful eating is about paying full attention to the experience of eating and drinking, both inside and outside the body. It starts with acknowledging the food on your plate. Take a moment to appreciate the colors, textures, and smells. This simple act of grace can set the stage for a more intentional and enjoyable dining experience.

When we eat mindfully, we engage all our senses. Touch the food with your hands, feel its texture, sense its temperature. Take small bites and chew slowly. Notice how the flavors unfold in your mouth. This practice not only enhances the enjoyment of food but can also aid in digestion, as the slower eating pace gives your stomach enough time to signal to your brain when it is full.

Practicing mindful eating can help us recognize and respond to hunger and satiety cues. Often, we eat out of habit or emotional triggers rather than actual hunger. By slowing down and paying attention, we can tune into our body's signals and make more intentional choices. Is your stomach growling, or are you reaching for that snack because you're bored or stressed?

Let's not forget to extend mindfulness to the process of preparing food. The act of cooking can become a meditative practice in itself. Focus on chopping vegetables, stirring pots, and measuring ingredients. Each task, when done with full attention, can bring a sense of peace and fulfillment. Notice the transformation of raw ingredients into a nourishing meal, and appreciate the effort and creativity that cooking requires.

Mindful eating also invites us to reflect on where our food comes from. Consider the journey of the ingredients on your plate—from the earth to the grocery store to your kitchen. Think about the farmers, the transporters, the stockers, and everyone involved in bringing the food to you. This reflection fosters gratitude and a deeper connection to the food you're eating.

One practice that can enhance mindful eating is to incorporate a brief pause before and after meals. Before eating, take a moment to breathe and center yourself. This pause can help transition your mind from whatever you were doing before to the act of eating. After your meal, sit quietly for a minute or two. Notice how your body feels. This post-meal reflection helps you tune into your body's response to the food.

Mindful eating isn't about making every meal a perfect experience. It's about increasing your awareness and making small, manageable changes over time. Maybe you start with breakfast or choose one meal per day to eat mindfully. The goal is progress, not perfection. By setting realistic expectations, you can cultivate a lasting mindful eating practice.

Consider keeping a food journal—not for counting calories, but for noting how foods make you feel. Record your hunger levels before you eat, what you ate, and how you felt after. This practice can reveal patterns and help you make more mindful choices. For example, you might notice that eating a heavy lunch makes you sluggish in the afternoon, prompting you to opt for lighter, more energizing foods instead.

Mindful eating can benefit not only your mental well-being but also your physical health. Studies have shown that mindful eating can aid in weight management, reduce binge eating, and improve overall nutrition. When we pay attention to what and how we eat, we are more likely to make healthier choices and savor our food rather than mindlessly consuming it.

If you encounter challenges—like eating mindfully at social gatherings or dealing with cravings—approach them with curiosity rather than judgment. Ask yourself what is driving your behavior in these situations. Is it social pressure, emotional comfort, or something else? By understanding the "why" behind your actions, you can develop more supportive strategies for eating mindfully in different contexts.

Sharing meals with others can also be an opportunity for mindfulness. Engage in conversations about the food you're eating, the memories it evokes, or the cultural traditions it represents. This not only enriches the dining experience but also fosters deeper connections with those around you.

Incorporating mindfulness into your eating habits doesn't require drastic lifestyle changes. Start small. Maybe begin with a mindful bite or a mindful sip of your morning coffee. Gradually, these moments can grow, taking root in your daily routine. Over time, mindful eating can become natural, offering you a deeper appreciation for food and the nourishment it provides.

Remember, the journey of mindful eating is continuous. There will be days when you eat on the go, skip meals, or indulge in mindless snacking. And that's okay. Mindfulness is about noticing these moments without judgment and gently steering yourself back on course. It's about creating a compassionate relationship with food and yourself.

Ultimately, mindful eating is more than a practice; it's a way of life. It's about bringing awareness and intention to one of the most fundamental aspects of human existence. By making the choice to eat mindfully, you are not only nurturing your body but also cultivating a deeper sense of peace and connection to the present moment.

Mindful Walking

Imagine your daily walk transformed into a journey of self-awareness and tranquility. Mindful walking is precisely that—an opportunity to infuse a mundane activity with profound mindfulness. It's about paying attention to each step, the movement of your body, and the sensations underfoot. In our hustle and bustle society, walking is often just a way to get from point A to B, but it can be so much more.

Mindful walking offers a bridge between formal meditation practice and everyday life. It involves cultivating mindfulness not just while sitting on a cushion, but while you're on the move. You're essentially bringing the principles of meditation into motion, which can be a powerful way to deepen your practice and bring a greater sense of presence into your daily activities.

So, how do you get started? It begins with intention. Set the intention to walk mindfully. This means choosing to be present with every step. You don't need any special equipment or a scenic route. You can practice mindful walking anywhere—on city sidewalks, in parks, or even in your own living room.

Begin by standing still. Take a moment to feel your body and your breath. Notice how your feet make contact with the ground. Feel the sensations in your legs and feet. Start walking at a natural pace, paying attention to the movement of your legs and the contact of your feet with the ground. Observe your surroundings with a sense of curiosity and openness, but keep your attention primarily on the sensations of walking.

One of the simplest techniques for mindful walking is to synchronize your steps with your breath. As you breathe in, take a few steps. As you breathe out, take a few steps. This rhythm can help anchor your mind in the present moment. If you notice your mind wandering—perhaps ruminating on the past or planning the future—gently bring your attention back to the feeling of your feet on the ground and the rhythm of your breath.

Mindful walking is also a wonderful practice for those who find sitting meditation challenging. It allows you to develop mindfulness while engaging in physical movement, which can be easier for some people. It provides a way to channel restless energy into a meditative practice.

Think of your walk as an exploration. What do you hear? What do you see? What do you smell? Engage all your senses. This sensory awareness can heighten your experience and keep you anchored in the present. Listen to the sound of birds or the rustle of leaves. Notice the color and texture of the path ahead. The more you immerse yourself in these sensory experiences, the more grounded you will feel.

But mindful walking is not just about pleasant sensations. It also involves becoming acutely aware of the sensations of discomfort or pain. Perhaps your back starts to ache or your feet feel tired. Instead of immediately trying to change these sensations, try observing them with curiosity. What do they feel like? How do they change with each step? This practice of non-reactive awareness can help build resilience and patience.

Mindful walking can be integrated into any part of your day. It doesn't need to be a separate activity. You can practice it during your commute, while running errands, or even walking your dog. The key is to bring mindfulness to the forefront of your attention, turning ordinary walks into opportunities for meditation.

Incorporating mindful walking into your daily routine can have wonderful benefits for your mental well-being. It's a gentle form of exercise that can reduce stress, improve mood, and increase overall mindfulness. Physically, it can help improve balance, coordination, and circulation. Spiritually, it can foster a deeper connection to yourself and the world around you.

To maintain consistency, you might set aside a specific time each day for mindful walking. Perhaps it's first thing in the morning or during your lunch break. You can also turn it into a ritual by choosing a special path or park that invites a sense of peace and reflection. As you make mindful walking a regular practice, you may find that it becomes a cherished part of your day—a time to reconnect with yourself and find solace in the simplicity of movement.

Additionally, mindful walking can be a communal activity. Walking with others in silence, each person attuned to their own experience, can create a collective sense of calm and mindfulness. This shared quietude can be deeply nourishing, fostering a sense of connection without the need for words. Group mindful walking meditations are becoming increasingly popular in various mindfulness communities, emphasizing the power of collective practice.

As you embrace mindful walking, remember that it's not about achieving a particular goal or state of mind. It's about the process of walking with awareness, bringing your attention back to your steps, breaths, and sensations whenever your mind drifts. The journey itself is the practice, and each step is a new opportunity to deepen your mindfulness.

In the end, mindful walking is a beautiful reminder that mindfulness doesn't require special conditions. You don't need a serene mountain retreat or a quiet room to be mindful. You can bring mindfulness into your every step, making your ordinary walk a pathway to peace, presence, and profound self-awareness.

Chapter 5: Overcoming Common Challenges

Embarking on your mindfulness journey is a commendable step, but it isn't always smooth sailing. You're bound to encounter hurdles like handling distractions and dealing with doubt. Maybe you sit down to meditate, but your mind buzzes with unfinished tasks or nagging worries—this is perfectly normal. Rather than seeing these challenges as barriers, view them as opportunities to deepen your practice. When distractions arise, gently guide your focus back to your breath or a chosen focal point. Doubt, whether it's about your ability to meditate or the efficacy of the practice, can also creep in. Instead of letting it derail you, acknowledge these feelings and remind yourself that every expert was once a beginner. By approaching these common challenges with patience and a sense of curiosity, you can transform obstacles into stepping stones, inching closer to a more mindful and fulfilling life.

Handling Distractions

Distractions are everywhere. They're like uninvited guests that just pop up, often at the worst times possible. Whether you're trying to meditate, work, or simply enjoy a quiet moment, distractions can derail your focus and throw you off balance. But here's the good news: by learning how to effectively handle distractions, you can improve your focus, reduce stress, and create a sense of peace and self-awareness in your daily life.

First things first, recognize that distractions are a natural part of life. You're not alone in facing them, and you're certainly not failing if your mind wanders now and then. It's all about how you respond to these distractions that makes the difference. The aim isn't to eliminate distractions completely—that's nearly impossible—but to find ways to minimize their impact on your mental well-being.

Start by identifying your most common distractions. Is it the constant ping of notifications on your phone? Or perhaps it's the chatter of coworkers or family members? Understanding what most frequently breaks your focus gives you the power to address it directly. You might find it helpful to keep a distraction journal for a week, noting down what distracts you and how often it happens. This can provide valuable insights into your distraction patterns and triggers.

Once you've identified the culprits, it's time to take action. For digital distractions, consider setting specific times to check your phone or social media accounts. You can use the "do not disturb" feature on your devices during critical periods of focus, such as meditation or work. Creating tech-free zones or times can also help. For instance, make your bedroom a phone-free area and commit to not using devices during meals.

Environmental adjustments can also play a significant role in handling distractions. If you're easily distracted by noise, noise-canceling headphones or a white noise machine can be a game-changer. Arrange your workspace to minimize visual distractions; keep it clutter-free and organized to avoid unnecessary interruptions. If possible, create a dedicated meditation or work space that signals to your brain that it's time to focus when you enter it.

Another effective strategy is to practice mindfulness itself. When a distraction occurs, instead of immediately reacting to it, observe it. Notice how your body and mind respond. Are you feeling anxious, annoyed, or curious? Acknowledging the distraction without judgment and gently bringing your focus back to your breath or task at hand can be incredibly powerful. This practice trains your mind to maintain focus and not get swept away by every passing distraction.

Mindfulness techniques such as the "noting" practice can be particularly helpful. When a distraction arises, label it with a simple word like "thinking," "hearing," or "feeling." This process of labeling can detach you from the distraction, turning it into a mere object of observation rather than a source of frustration. After labeling, gently guide your attention back to your breath or whatever task you're focused on.

Time management also plays a crucial role in managing distractions. Break your day into focused work intervals with short breaks in between—a technique known as the Pomodoro Technique. During these focused periods, commit to working on one task without allowing distractions. Use the breaks to mindfully relax, stretch, or take a brief walk. This approach not only improves productivity but also makes room for moments of mindfulness throughout the day, which can enhance overall well-being.

Physical self-care can't be overlooked, either. A well-rested, nourished, and hydrated body is less prone to distractions. Make sure you're getting enough sleep, eating a balanced diet, and staying hydrated. Incorporate regular physical activity into your routine, as exercise can improve focus and reduce stress, making it easier to handle distractions when they arise.

Sometimes, handling distractions is about addressing the underlying issues causing your mind to wander. Stress, anxiety, and unresolved emotions can be significant sources of distraction. Incorporating practices such as journaling, talking to a trusted friend, or seeking professional help when needed can provide clarity and alleviate some of the mental clutter that leads to distractions.

And remember, it's okay to be kind to yourself during this process. Handling distractions is a skill that takes time and practice to develop. Celebrate small victories when you notice an improvement in your focus or when you successfully navigate through a distracting situation. Recognize that every moment spent in focused attention, no matter how small, is a step towards greater mental well-being.

In a world full of distractions, cultivating the ability to manage them can transform your life. Imagine what you can achieve with enhanced focus and less stress. By consistently applying these strategies and maintaining a mindful approach, you can build resilience against distractions and pave the way to a more peaceful, productive, and fulfilling life.

Dealing with Doubt

Let's face it, doubt is something we all encounter, especially when stepping into new and unfamiliar territories like mindfulness and meditation. It's completely natural to question whether you're doing it right, if it's worth the effort, or if you'll ever see the benefits everyone keeps raving about. In fact, these doubts can act as stumbling blocks, making it easy to throw in the towel before reaping the rewards that mindfulness can bring. But what if I told you that doubt itself can be an opportunity for growth? Yes, you heard it right. Doubt isn't necessarily a dead end; it can be a stepping stone if navigated wisely.

Firstly, it's crucial to acknowledge and accept your doubts rather than brushing them aside. The very essence of mindfulness is to observe your thoughts and emotions without judgment. By confronting your doubts head-on, you create a space where they can be examined and understood. Ignoring them only gives them more power. Imagine sitting with your doubt as if it's an old friend who's come over for a chat. Listen, understand, but don't let it dictate your actions. This act of mindful acknowledgment, strangely enough, can reduce the grip that doubt has on your mind.

Often, doubt stems from a perfectionist mindset. You might think there is a "right" way to meditate or practice mindfulness. Newsflash: there isn't. Mindfulness is highly personal, and there is no one-size-fits-all approach. It's okay if your mind wanders during meditation or if you don't feel an immediate sense of peace. These experiences are part of the journey. By releasing the need for perfection, you open yourself to a more authentic experience that's unique to you. Remember, it's about progress, not perfection.

An excellent way to deal with doubt is by incorporating a "beginner's mind" approach. A term borrowed from Zen Buddhism, a beginner's mind means approaching each session with an open, curious attitude as if it's your first time. This mindset can help dissolve preconceived notions and set expectations aside. When you reduce the mental clutter of "shoulds" and "oughts," you free yourself to experience mindfulness practice in its pure form.

Accountability can also be a powerful tool in overcoming doubt. Connect with a friend, join a mindfulness group, or participate in a guided meditation class. Sharing your experiences and hearing others' stories can provide a sense of community and validation. You're not alone in your journey; many others are walking the same path and facing similar challenges. Community support can offer encouragement and new perspectives that can help you stay motivated and committed.

Doubt can also be mitigated by setting realistic, achievable goals. Instead of aiming for an hour-long meditation session right off the bat, start with just five or ten minutes. As you meet these smaller, manageable goals, your confidence will grow, and so will your practice. Small wins can counteract the negativity that doubt brings, turning it into a more manageable and temporary state of mind.

Another practical technique is journaling. Document your thoughts, emotions, and experiences related to your mindfulness journey. Over time, you'll likely notice patterns and progress that can help dispel doubts. Writing down your experiences makes them tangible and provides a reflective surface where you can see growth that might not be immediately apparent in day-to-day practice. Your journal acts as evidence of your journey, validating your efforts and counteracting doubts.

Let's not forget the aspect of gratitude. Keeping a gratitude journal can shift your focus from what's going wrong to what's going right. Each time you note something you're grateful for, you're training your brain to recognize and appreciate positive experiences. This can counterbalance the negative impact of doubt, helping you develop a more positive and resilient mindset over time.

Lastly, consider the role of self-compassion in dealing with doubt. Everyone faces challenges and setbacks. Treat yourself with the same kindness and understanding that you would offer a friend. If you miss a meditation session or find your mind wandering more than you'd like, practice self-compassion.

Remind yourself that mindfulness is a journey, not a destination, and every step you take, no matter how small, is a move forward.

In conclusion, doubt is a common visitor in the realm of mindfulness and meditation. It's not a sign of failure but an invitation to deepen your practice. By acknowledging your doubts, adjusting your mindset, seeking community, setting achievable goals, documenting your journey, practicing gratitude, and embracing self-compassion, you can turn doubt from a roadblock into a catalyst for growth. Embrace it, learn from it, and let it propel you towards a richer, more mindful life.

Chapter 6: Guided Meditations for Beginners

Starting your meditation journey with guided meditations can be a game-changer, especially if you're new to the practice. Picture this: you're sitting comfortably, headphones on, and a soothing voice leads you step-by-step through the meditation process. It's like having a personal coach in your ear, making the path to relaxation and mindfulness much more accessible. For beginners, this structure removes the guesswork and helps you stay focused, reducing the likelihood of your mind wandering off. Guided meditations often involve visualization or specific breathing techniques that can quickly transport you to a calmer state of mind. Whether you're tackling a body scan to tune into physical sensations or a simple relaxation meditation to melt away stress, these guided sessions are designed to ease you into a consistent practice, setting a solid foundation for deeper experiences down the road. By following along with these sessions, you'll soon notice an increase in your ability to focus and a greater sense of peace, making them an invaluable resource on your path to mental well-being.

Relaxation Meditation

In our fast-paced world, finding a moment of peace can often feel like an insurmountable challenge. That's where relaxation meditation comes into play. This form of meditation, ideal for beginners, helps us create a sanctuary of calm amidst the chaos. It's like taking a gentle reset for your mind and body, allowing you to disengage from stress and find a slice of tranquility.

Relaxation meditation doesn't demand any special skills or equipment. All you need is a quiet space and a willingness to let go. You can practice it sitting up, lying down, or even reclined in a comfortable chair. The primary goal is to encourage your muscles to relax and your mind to drift into a state of calm awareness. Think of it as giving yourself permission to just be.

To start, find your quiet space and settle in comfortably. Close your eyes and take a few deep breaths. Feel your body anchored to the ground or the chair you're sitting in. Pay attention to how your breath feels as it flows in and out. These initial moments are meant to center you and prepare your mind for deeper relaxation.

Next, begin a slow and deliberate body scan. Starting from the top of your head, mentally note each part of your body. Consciously relax your forehead, your eyes, your jaw, and so on. Work your way down to your toes, releasing tension as you go. This process not only helps in physically relaxing your muscles but also shifts your focus away from daily stresses and towards the present moment.

Many people find that incorporating a mantra or positive affirmation can deepen their relaxation. This could be a simple word like "peace" or a short phrase like "I am calm." Repeat it quietly in your mind, aligning it with your breath. Each repetition serves as a gentle reminder to let go of stress and embrace serenity.

It's perfectly normal for your mind to wander during relaxation meditation. Thoughts may pop up about your to-do list, worries, or even what's for dinner. When this happens, gently guide your attention back to your breath or your chosen mantra. Don't judge yourself or your thoughts—simply acknowledge them and let them pass.

Visualization is another effective technique in relaxation meditation. Picture yourself in a place that signifies peace to you. It could be a secluded beach, a quiet forest, or a sunny meadow. Envision the sights, sounds, and smells of this place. Allow yourself to be fully immersed in the experience. The more vividly you can picture it, the more powerfully it can anchor your mind in tranquility.

One key aspect of relaxation meditation is recognizing the ebb and flow of your thoughts without getting caught up in them. You might imagine your thoughts as clouds drifting across a clear sky. Notice them, but don't chase them. This practice helps build a mental resilience that can be incredibly effective in managing everyday stress.

To bring your relaxation meditation to a close, start to bring a gentle awareness back to your physical surroundings. Wiggle your fingers and toes, stretch your body lightly, and take a few deep breaths. Open your eyes slowly and take a moment to appreciate the calm you've cultivated. Notice how your body feels lighter and your mind clearer.

Implementing relaxation meditation into your daily routine can yield significant benefits. Even dedicating just ten minutes a day can make a noticeable difference. Over time, you may find that you handle stress more effectively and approach life's challenges with a newfound sense of calm.

Consistency is key when it comes to meditation. While you may not feel immediate results, with regular practice, the benefits will become more apparent. Think of each session as a building block—each time you practice, you're laying the foundation for a more peaceful and focused mind.

Don't hesitate to experiment with different techniques within relaxation meditation. Perhaps you find that you prefer guided meditations or calming music in the background. There are numerous apps and online resources available that offer a variety of guided sessions tailored to relaxation. Feel free to explore these options to find what resonates best with you.

Remember, the essence of relaxation meditation is to give yourself the gift of stillness. In a world that demands constant motion and attention, taking a moment to pause and breathe is an act of self-care. It's a conscious choice to prioritize your mental and emotional well-being, even if just for a few minutes each day.

Consider integrating relaxation meditation with other mindfulness practices as you progress. The skills and calmness you cultivate here can enhance other forms of meditation and mindfulness in your daily life. Whether paired with mindful walking, eating, or simply being present, the ripple effects of relaxation meditation can touch all areas of your life.

Making relaxation meditation a regular part of your routine may also inspire those around you. Your sense of calm can be infectious, showing friends and family the value of taking time for themselves too. You may even become a source of support and guidance as others begin their own meditation journeys.

The accessibility and simplicity of relaxation meditation make it an ideal starting point in the world of mindfulness. As you become more comfortable with this practice, you might find yourself eager to explore other meditation techniques and dive deeper into the benefits they offer. But for now, relish the peace and relaxation you've cultivated in these moments. They are a testament to your commitment to a healthier, more mindful you.

Body Scan Meditation

Embarking on a body scan meditation can be a transformative experience, especially if you're new to mindfulness practices. Think of it as a comprehensive check-in with your own body, allowing you to foster a deeper connection with yourself from head to toe. This guided meditation invites you to slow down, tune in, and cultivate a sense of presence that can ripple into every aspect of your life.

It all begins with finding a comfortable place to sit or lie down. You don't need any special equipment—just a quiet space where you won't be disturbed for a little while. You can sit on a chair with your feet flat on the ground or lie down on a yoga mat or even your bed. Close your eyes, and bring your attention to your breath, letting it flow naturally without trying to control it.

Start by noticing the sensations at the top of your head. Imagine you're slowly scanning each part of your body, moving down from your scalp to your forehead, your eyes, and then your cheeks. There's no rush. Allow yourself to simply observe without judgment. Feel any tension or relaxation in each area.

As you continue, bring your attention to your neck and shoulders. These areas often harbor a lot of stress, and acknowledging this tension is the first step toward releasing it. Simply notice, without trying to change anything. Allow yourself to just be.

Next, shift your focus to your arms, moving down from your upper arms to your elbows, forearms, wrists, and finally your hands and fingers. Feel the weight of your arms, the warmth or coolness of your skin, and any other sensations that arise. If your mind starts to wander—which it most certainly will—gently guide it back to the area you're focusing on.

Moving your awareness to your chest, feel the rise and fall of your breath. Notice your heartbeat, the expansion of your ribs, and the simple act of breathing. Allow these feelings to be a reminder of your aliveness. Without needing to alter anything, just be with what is.

As you move down to your abdomen, observe the sensations of digestion or tension. This area can be a repository for stress, so take extra care to be gentle with yourself. If you find discomfort, acknowledge it with kindness.

Next, bring your focus to your hips and pelvic area, areas that are often overlooked but carry vital connections to our sense of grounding and stability. As you scan through these parts, bring a sense of gratitude for the strength and support they provide.

Moving awareness to your legs, start at your thighs and move down to your knees, your shins, your ankles, and finally your feet and toes. Notice the textures, the points of contact with the ground, and any sensations of weight or pressure. Your legs carry you through life; take a moment to appreciate their effort.

Throughout this scan, remember that it's perfectly normal for your mind to wander. When it does, acknowledge that it's happened, and gently bring your focus back to where you left off. The act of returning your focus is itself a crucial part of the meditation, training your mind to remain present.

A body scan meditation isn't about achieving complete stillness or eradicating thoughts. Instead, it's an exercise in awareness and non-judgmental observation. Over time, this practice can help you become more attuned to physical sensations and signals, which are often early indicators of stress or imbalance.

Finish your body scan by taking a few more deep breaths, in through the nose and out through the mouth, slowly bringing your attention back to the room around you. When you're ready, open your eyes. Take note of how you feel, both physically and mentally. This pause provides a moment of reflection and gratitude.

Incorporating body scan meditation into your routine can lead to numerous benefits. It can reduce physical tension, improve emotional regulation, and enhance your overall sense of well-being. It's a way to befriend your body and listen to what it has to tell you.

Don't be discouraged if this practice feels difficult at first. Like any skill, it takes time to develop. With consistent practice, you'll likely find it easier to stay focused and present. You may even notice subtle shifts in how you relate to your body and your experiences throughout the day.

Each time you practice the body scan, you're building a foundation of mindfulness that will support you in other areas of life. It's a gentle yet profound way to cultivate a sense of peace and awareness, fostering a deeper connection with yourself and your surroundings.

So, embrace this journey with patience and compassion. Take it one moment at a time, and let the body scan be an anchor in your mindfulness practice. The benefits may extend far beyond the meditation itself, enriching your daily life in ways you might not have imagined.

Chapter 7: Deepening Your Practice

Deepening your practice involves taking those initial steps you're already familiar with—like setting up a meditation space and selecting techniques—and supercharging them for greater impact. To truly integrate mindfulness into your daily life, start by gradually extending your meditation time. It might feel like a stretch at first, but trust that with persistence, it will become as effortless as breathing. Exploring advanced techniques can also open new avenues of awareness and calm. These approaches won't just help you meditate longer; they'll deepen the quality of your focus, making every session richer and more rewarding. This chapter isn't just about spending more time with your eyes closed; it's about expanding your inner horizons and discovering the depths of mindfulness that might have seemed elusive before.

Extending Meditation Time

Alright, so you've been meditating for a bit now and you're feeling the itch to go deeper. Extending your meditation time can be an incredibly rewarding way to deepen your practice, giving you more space to explore your inner landscape and connect with yourself on a profound level. But like any good thing, extending your meditation time requires both strategy and patience.

First things first, let's talk logistics. You might be thinking, "How do I fit longer meditation sessions into my busy schedule?" Start small. If you're used to meditating for 10 minutes, try extending it to 15. Small increments can make the process manageable and less intimidating. You can also look at it as a gradual training process for your mind and body. Gradually extending the time spent in meditation allows your nervous system to adapt, which is crucial for maintaining a sustainable practice.

Next, consider the timing. Morning might be the best for some people because the mind is still fresh and uncluttered from the day's events. Others might find evening meditation more relaxing, serving as a buffer to unwind from the day's stress. Experiment to see what works best for you.

Environment is another critical factor. A quiet, comfortable place free from distractions can make it easier to extend your meditation sessions. Consider upgrading your meditation space with items that make you feel more at ease—think cozy cushions, soft lighting, or even a gentle timer that doesn't jolt you out of your meditation abruptly.

Now, let's be honest. Sitting for an extended period can be uncomfortable. Your legs may go numb, your back might ache, thoughts will wander—this is all normal. Instead of seeing these as obstacles, view them as opportunities for mindfulness. Physical discomfort can be a powerful point of focus. Feel the tension in your body. Observe it. Lean into it with curiosity rather than resistance. This practice not only extends your meditation time but also enhances your ability to stay mindful in challenging situations outside of meditation.

One effective technique to help expand your meditation session is to break it into segments. For example, start with 5 minutes of breath awareness, move to 10 minutes of body scanning, then spend the last 10 minutes in open awareness. This segmentation can make longer sessions feel more dynamic and less daunting.

It's also useful to set an intention before you begin. This doesn't have to be anything grand. Simply acknowledging why you're extending your meditation can help to ground your practice. Whether it's to foster greater emotional resilience, enhance focus, or simply enjoy a deeper sense of peace, your intention can act as a guidepost throughout the session.

Engaging with a meditation community can also be incredibly supportive. Sometimes, the motivation to extend your practice can wane if you're going at it alone. Joining a local meditation group or an online community can offer both accountability and inspiration. Listening to others' experiences can provide new insights and approaches that you might not have considered.

Patience and self-compassion are your allies in this journey. Extending your meditation time isn't a race. It's perfectly fine to have days when you can't sit as long as you'd planned. Life happens. Be kind to yourself and remember that the quality of your mindfulness is more important than the length of time spent meditating.

Let's not forget the mental barriers. When extending your meditation time, it's common to encounter a barrage of thoughts questioning your effort. "Am I doing this right?" "Is this even worth it?" These thoughts are part of the process. Sit with them, observe them, and gently bring your focus back to your chosen point of awareness. Over time, you'll find your internal dialogue becoming more supportive and less intrusive.

If you're really struggling with time extension, guided meditations tailored for longer sessions can be a great tool. These can offer structure and keep your mind engaged, making it easier to sit for longer periods. There are plenty of apps and online resources where you can find guided meditations geared towards extended practice.

Practice patience and persistence. Like any skill, extending your meditation time gets easier with consistent effort. Make it a gradual process, and allow room for both setbacks and progress. Each session is a new opportunity to deepen your connection with yourself.

As you start to meditate for longer periods, you might notice subtle changes. Maybe you'll feel a deeper sense of tranquility or an enhanced ability to focus throughout your day. These are the fruits of your labor, small but significant shifts that signal you're on the right path.

In sum, extending your meditation time can profoundly deepen your practice and deliver richer rewards. It's a journey that requires a mix of patience, curiosity, and a willingness to face discomfort head-on. Embrace it slowly, keep experimenting, and let your practice evolve naturally. The deeper you go, the more you'll discover about yourself, and that's a journey worth taking.

Exploring Advanced Techniques

So, you've got the basics down. You've found your meditation groove, you're tuning into your breath, and maybe you've even noticed some positive changes taking place. But what happens next? Well, that's where we bring in the advanced techniques. These methods aren't just for seasoned meditators; they're for anyone ready to deepen their practice and access new layers of mindfulness and awareness.

One of the first advanced techniques you might explore is the concept of *non-judgmental observation.* While it sounds simple, it's one of the most challenging aspects to master. Instead of labeling thoughts and feelings as "good" or "bad," this technique encourages you to simply observe them as they are. It's about allowing yourself to experience thoughts and emotions without attaching any value or narrative to them. Embracing this practice can lead to a profound shift in how you relate to your inner world.

Another powerful technique is *loving-kindness meditation* (often referred to as Metta meditation). At its heart, this practice is about sending good wishes and compassion first to yourself, then to loved ones, acquaintances, and even those with whom you have conflicts. You begin by silently repeating phrases like "May I be happy," "May I be healthy," directing positive energy toward yourself. Then, progressively extend these wishes outward. This technique can be incredibly transformative, fostering a greater sense of connection and empathy with others.

Next, consider diving into the practice of **shadow work**. Rooted in Jungian psychology, shadow work involves acknowledging and integrating the parts of ourselves that we often keep hidden—the aspects we're ashamed of or haven't fully explored. This isn't about self-criticism but about compassionate self-inquiry. By understanding and embracing our shadows, we become whole, and our mindfulness practice deepens as a result.

Advanced practitioners might also engage in *longer retreats*, which offer extended periods of silence and meditation. These retreats, ranging from a few days to several weeks, provide a unique opportunity to disconnect from the daily hustle and delve deeper into mindfulness. The rhythm of a retreat often supports more intensive practice, leading to breakthroughs and insights that might take much longer to achieve in a daily practice setting. Even if you're not ready for a multi-week commitment, a weekend retreat can offer a taste of the profound states of awareness possible.

Another powerful technique involves *combining breathwork with body scans*. By integrating focused breathing exercises with systematic attention to different body parts, you can unlock deeper states of relaxation and awareness. This combination can be particularly effective in releasing stored tension and facilitating emotional release. It's like hitting the reset button for both your mind and body.

And let's not overlook the practice of *mindful self-inquiry*. This involves asking yourself open-ended questions during meditation, such as "Who am I?" or "What do I need right now?" Without the pressure to find immediate answers, this technique invites curiosity and deeper introspection. Over time, it can lead to greater self-awareness and a clearer understanding of your inner motivations and desires.

Another advanced technique that can elevate your practice is the use of *mantras*. While some beginners might use mantras to help focus their meditation, advanced practitioners delve deeper into the vibrational quality of specific sounds or phrases. In many traditions, mantras are considered to carry specific energetic frequencies that can assist in healing, focus, and transcending the ordinary states of consciousness. Next time you meditate, consider experimenting with a mantra and observe how it shifts your experience.

Let's talk about **visualization** as an advanced tool. While simple visualizations might help beginners ease into meditation, advanced practitioners can use visualization to explore complex emotional landscapes or to project themselves into future scenarios. For example, visualizing a peaceful place can help you access deep states of relaxation, while visualizing your goals can potentiate your efforts to achieve them. These visual journeys can be potent catalysts for growth and healing.

Another avenue worth exploring is the practice of *alternative nostril breathing*, or Nadi Shodhana. This pranayama technique balances the left and right hemispheres of the brain, fostering a sense of calm and mental clarity. It's especially beneficial if you find yourself struggling with decision-making or feeling mentally cluttered. The rhythmic nature of this practice can also deepen your experience, making each meditation session more enriching.

For those who crave a challenge, **yoga nidra** is a hypnotic-like form of meditation that guides you into a state of conscious sleep. It's perfect for those days when you feel drained but still want to meditate. As you lie down and follow guided instructions, your body enters a sleep-like state while your mind remains aware. It's an incredible way to restore your energy and foster deep relaxation without actually falling asleep.

We can't talk about advanced techniques without mentioning the *practice of silence*, or mauna, which involves not just external but also internal silence. Setting aside periods for silence can be revolutionary. This practice isn't just about not speaking; it's about quieting the mind's chatter to listen more deeply internally. You might designate a day each week for this practice or incorporate it into a retreat experience. The resulting stillness can make your other mindfulness practices more resonant and effective.

Similarly, *mindfulness of emotions* can take an advanced approach. Rather than just noting an emotion and letting it go, this technique invites you to dive deep into the emotion's nuances—the physical sensations it brings, the thoughts it provokes, and the memories it might be linked to. By gently exploring these dimensions, you can better understand and integrate your emotional experiences, making them less overwhelming in daily life.

Last but certainly not least, incorporating *rituals* into your mindfulness practice can provide another layer of depth. Rituals offer structure and meaning, making each meditation session feel like a sacred act. Whether it's lighting a candle, using essential oils, or saying a specific prayer before meditating, these little acts can help signal to your mind that it's time to transition into a state of mindfulness. Such ritualistic elements can bring a comforting and grounding aspect to your practice, making it easier to slip into deeper states of awareness.

Exploring these advanced techniques may seem overwhelming at first, but the key is to go at your own pace. Pick one or two practices that resonate with you and integrate them slowly. Each technique has its unique beauty and can contribute significantly to deepening your practice. The journey might be challenging, but rest assured, it's deeply rewarding.

Remember, there's no finish line in mindfulness. As you delve into these advanced techniques, you aren't striving for perfection but rather a richer, fuller understanding of yourself and the world around you. Let curiosity and kindness guide your explorations, and you'll find that the pathways to deeper mindfulness are limitless.

Chapter 8: Using Mindfulness to Reduce Stress

Stress, in various forms, is an inevitable part of our daily lives, but incorporating mindfulness can provide a profound antidote. Practicing mindfulness enables us to anchor ourselves in the present moment, allowing us to observe our thoughts and emotions without judgment. This non-reactive awareness diminishes the power stressors hold over us, leading to a calmer mind and alleviated tension. By recognizing the triggers and employing mindful breathing or body scan techniques, we can interrupt the automatic stress response, creating space for intentional, soothing reactions. Transform your stress into a gateway for inner peace, and you'll notice the ripple effects spreading throughout all aspects of your life.

Identifying Triggers

We've covered a lot in this journey of using mindfulness to reduce stress. Now, let's dive into a critical aspect that often goes unnoticed yet plays a huge role in our stress levels: identifying our triggers. Triggers are those sneaky, often subconscious, elements in our environment or thoughts that ignite our stress responses. Once we learn to spot them, we can take proactive steps to manage them effectively.

To start, try to tune into your emotional state throughout the day. Keep tabs on moments when you feel your stress levels rising, your heart pounding, or your mind racing. Is it during your commute, when you read emails, or maybe when you're faced with a tight deadline? Recognizing these moments gives you valuable data. This isn't just about pointing fingers at external circumstances but understanding the interplay between your environment and your internal reactions.

For some people, stress triggers can be as obvious as loud noises or traffic jams. For others, they might be more subtle, like a particular tone of voice or an unfinished task list. Mindfulness helps us become more aware of these triggers. When you start observing without judgment, you create a mental space where you can respond rather than react.

Here's a practical tip: start a stress journal. Jot down moments when you feel stressed and note what was happening just before the stress hit. Was it an unexpected request from your boss or a family member's remark that threw you off balance? Writing this down creates a record that helps you see patterns over time.

Another effective approach is to focus on your body. Often, our bodies react to stress before our minds can catch up. Maybe your shoulders tense up, your stomach feels uneasy, or you get a headache. Paying attention to these physical signals can provide clues about your triggers, allowing you to address them more skillfully.

It's also worthwhile to explore deeper, more ingrained triggers. These could be rooted in past experiences or long-standing habits. Maybe you've internalized certain expectations or fears that activate your stress response when certain situations arise. Mindfulness helps us peel back these layers gently, giving us a clearer view of what truly affects us.

Understanding your triggers is an ongoing process, not a one-time event. It's like peeling an onion – you discover more layers as you go. Simply being aware is a huge first step, but don't stop there. Actively work on strategies to manage or avoid these triggers when possible. This could mean setting boundaries, changing your environment, or even altering your perspective.

Incorporate this awareness into your daily mindfulness practice. During meditation, instead of pushing away thoughts that arise, observe them. Are certain recurring themes causing your mind to wander? These could likely point to hidden triggers. Your meditation practice becomes a safe space to explore these triggers without the immediate need to act on them.

You can also use mindfulness to decondition your responses to certain triggers. Let's say the sound of your phone pinging with a new message always makes you anxious. Practice taking a deep breath each time you hear it. Over time, you might find that this once-stressful trigger loses its power over you.

And remember, not all triggers are within our control. However, recognizing what they are gives us a chance to change how we respond. If you can't change a triggering situation, you can always use mindfulness to change your reaction to it. This shift from 'reacting' to 'responding' can significantly reduce your overall stress.

Don't be too hard on yourself if this feels challenging at first. It's perfectly normal. What's important is that you're taking steps to understand yourself better. Each small recognition and adjustment you make contributes to a larger shift towards a more peaceful and self-aware life.

So, be patient and compassionate with yourself. This journey of identifying triggers is just another part of your broader mindfulness practice. With persistent effort and mindful attention, you can transform these stressors into opportunities for growth and resilience.

Stress-Relief Techniques

The journey towards reducing stress through mindfulness often starts with simple, yet profoundly effective techniques. When stress overwhelms, these techniques can serve as anchors, pulling us back into the present moment and providing a sense of calm and clarity.

One of the most straightforward methods is the practice of **mindful breathing**. When you find yourself in a stressful situation, take a moment to pause and focus on your breath. Inhale deeply through your nose, hold for a few seconds, and then exhale slowly through your mouth. This simple act of mindful breathing can activate the parasympathetic nervous system, which helps the body return to a state of relaxation.

Another technique involves *progressive muscle relaxation.* This method requires you to focus on one muscle group at a time, tensing the muscles as you breathe in and slowly relaxing them as you breathe out. Start from your toes and work your way up to your head. This not only helps in releasing physical tension but also brings awareness to areas of the body that often hold stress.

Body scan meditation is another powerful technique for stress relief. Lie down comfortably and bring your attention to different parts of your body, starting from your toes and moving up to your head. As you scan each part of your body, notice any areas of tension or discomfort without trying to change them. Just bring your awareness to them. This practice helps in identifying hidden stressors that manifest physically within the body.

Engaging in *mindful walking* is another way to reduce stress. Take a stroll in a park or any quiet place. Walk slowly and deliberately, paying attention to the sensation of your feet touching the ground, the rhythm of your breath, and the sights and sounds around you. The act of mindfully walking can help ground your thoughts and make you feel more connected to the present.

Ever tried **mindful listening**? It involves paying full attention to sounds in your environment without any judgment. Find a quiet space, close your eyes, and just listen. It could be the rustling of leaves, distant chatter, or the hum of a refrigerator. This practice can help shift your focus away from stress-inducing thoughts and bring you into a state of peaceful awareness.

Guided imagery is another technique that many find useful. Close your eyes and imagine a place where you feel completely at peace, like a beach, a forest, or even a cozy spot in your home. Engage all your senses in the visualization—feel the warmth of the sun, hear the waves crashing, or smell the fresh pine. This immersive experience can provide a mental escape from stress and create a sense of tranquility.

A simple yet effective technique is **journaling**. Take a few minutes each day to write down your thoughts and feelings. Journaling allows you to process emotions, reflect on experiences, and gain perspective on what may be causing you stress. This form of expression can be incredibly cathartic and clarifying.

Engaging your creative side through *art mindfulness* can also be beneficial.

Activities like coloring, painting, or sketching can serve as a meditative practice that calms the mind. The act of creating art focuses your attention and can be a great way to express emotions that are difficult to articulate.

Incorporating **mindfulness into daily routines** is key. Simple actions like mindful eating—paying attention to the texture, flavor, and aroma of your food—can make every meal a mini-meditation session. Similarly, transforming routine activities like showering or washing dishes into mindful practices can help embed mindfulness into your everyday life, reducing overall stress.

Gratitude practice is also an excellent stress-relief technique. Take a moment each day to write down or mentally acknowledge things you're grateful for. This can shift your focus from what's causing stress to what brings joy and fulfillment.

Engaging in **mindful stretching or yoga** can release physical tension and improve mental clarity. Practices like yoga integrate breath control, meditation, and poses to promote relaxation and reduce stress. Even a few minutes of mindful stretching can help lift your spirits and enhance your focus.

Lastly, cultivating a *mindful mindset* toward technology use can significantly reduce stress. Establishing tech-free zones or times during your day can help you unplug and reconnect with yourself and your surroundings. When using technology, practice doing it mindfully, fully engaging with the task at hand rather than multitasking.

Integrating these stress-relief techniques into your life doesn't require grand gestures or extensive time commitments. What matters is consistency and the willingness to make mindfulness a part of your daily routine. As you explore these techniques, you'll discover a greater sense of peace and better tools to handle life's inevitable stresses. Remember, the goal isn't to eliminate stress completely but to develop a toolkit that allows you to navigate it more effectively.

These techniques form a solid foundation for reducing stress through mindfulness and can greatly enhance your mental well-being. Practice them regularly, and you'll likely find that peace and clarity become more readily available, helping to buffer against the stresses of everyday life.

53

Chapter 9: Improving Focus with Meditation

Meditation isn't just about finding peace—it's a powerful tool to sharpen your concentration too. Imagine your mind as a cluttered desk; meditation helps you clear it, so you can focus on the task at hand with laser-like precision. When you consistently practice meditation, it trains your brain to improve its attention span and reduce the tendencies to drift off into distractions. You don't need to sit for hours in a lotus position; even a few minutes of mindful breathing can make a significant difference. By incorporating techniques like focused attention and mantra repetition, you create a mental space where distractions fade, and clarity emerges. This newfound focus spills over into your daily life, making mundane tasks more manageable and complex challenges less daunting. So, embrace meditation not just for stillness but as a way to harness your mind's full potential.

Techniques for Sharpening Concentration

A fundamental aspect of meditation is its capacity to enhance concentration, allowing us to bring a more focused and calm presence into our daily lives. If you find that your attention often wanders, or that distractions seem to pull you in every direction, you're not alone. Thankfully, through dedicated practice, you can train your mind to become more still and attentive. Let's dive into several techniques specifically designed to hone your concentration.

Focused Attention Meditation

One of the most straightforward ways to improve concentration is through focused attention meditation. This technique involves selecting a single point of focus—such as your breath, a candle flame, or a simple object—and directing your full attention to it. When your mind inevitably wanders, gently bring it back to your chosen focal point. Over time, this practice helps to build your mind's ability to stay focused for longer periods.

Start with just a few minutes a day, gradually increasing the duration as your ability to concentrate strengthens. Some days will be easier than others, and that's perfectly normal. The key is consistency and patience.

Mantra Meditation

Mantra meditation employs a word or phrase that you repeat to yourself, either silently or aloud. The sound acts as an anchor for your mind, providing a stable point to return to whenever distractions arise. This method can be particularly helpful for those who struggle to keep their thoughts from wandering when meditating in silence.

Choose a mantra that resonates with you; it could be as simple as the word "peace" or a phrase like "I am calm." Repeating the mantra helps to steady your mind and bring it back to a state of focus. Over time, you'll likely find it easier to maintain concentration in other areas of your life as well.

Body Scan Meditation

Body scan meditation can also be an effective way to sharpen concentration. This practice involves mentally scanning each part of your body, from head to toe, noticing sensations and bringing awareness to areas of tension or discomfort. While it might seem counterintuitive, focusing on physical sensations can actually help train your mind to maintain a single-pointed focus.

This technique not only sharpens concentration but also promotes bodily awareness and relaxation. It's a two-for-one deal: improved focus and less stress.

Counting Meditation

Counting can be another useful technique to enhance concentration. You could count your breaths, counting up to ten and then starting over, or you could count down from one hundred. Focusing on numbers can keep your mind engaged and less likely to wander. Each time you catch yourself drifting, you simply return to the task at hand.

While it might sound simple, don't underestimate the effectiveness of counting meditation. It's incredibly straightforward, yet it packs a powerful punch in enhancing your focus.

Guided Meditation

If you're new to meditation or find it easier to maintain focus with some external guidance, guided meditation might be the way to go. In a guided session, an instructor provides verbal cues to help you stay on track. This could be in the form of live instruction, recorded audio, or video. The facilitator's voice serves as an external focal point, making it easier to maintain concentration.

Guided meditation sessions often incorporate visualization techniques, which can help anchor your attention and deepen your practice. Imagine yourself in a peaceful landscape or envision a soothing light filling your body. By engaging your imagination, you create a richer experience that can make it easier to maintain concentration.

Mindful Walking

Though it might seem paradoxical, moving meditations like mindful walking can also enhance concentration. Instead of sitting still, you focus on the sensations of walking—how your feet touch the ground, the movement of your legs, the rhythm of your breath. Mindful walking provides a dynamic focal point, which some people find easier to stick with.

Next time you find yourself overwhelmed or stressed, take a few minutes to practice mindful walking. It's a great way to incorporate mindfulness into your daily routine and sharpen your focus simultaneously.

Sensory Awareness

Building concentration through sensory awareness involves focusing intently on any of your five senses. This could be the sound of a bell, the taste of a piece of fruit, the texture of fabric, or the scent of an essential oil. Engaging your senses provides a rich and diverse range of focal points, helping to train your mind to become more adaptable and attentive.

To practice this, select a sensory object or experience, and dedicate a few minutes to observing it fully. Notice the details you might typically overlook. This practice can help to heighten your overall sensory awareness and improve your ability to concentrate.

Creative Focus Techniques

Incorporating creativity into your focus practice can be both fun and effective. Try drawing, painting, or even crafting as a form of meditation. Focus solely on the act of creation without worrying about the outcome. This form of meditation can cultivate a flow state, where your concentration naturally deepens as you become fully immersed in your activity.

If you're a writer, consider free-writing as a meditative exercise. Set a timer for a few minutes and write nonstop, focusing on the act of putting words on paper without judgment. This practice can improve mental clarity and concentration in a way that's both productive and enjoyable.

Breath Control Techniques

Finally, breath control techniques like Pranayama can be particularly effective in improving concentration. These exercises involve controlling your breath in specific ways to calm the mind and center your attention. Techniques like alternate nostril breathing or the 4-7-8 breath can help create a sense of balance and focus.

By spending just a few minutes each day on breath control, you can significantly enhance your ability to maintain concentration, both during meditation and in your everyday activities. Breath control techniques also offer the added benefit of reducing stress and promoting overall well-being.

Improving your focus through meditation is a gradual process that requires commitment and patience. However, the rewards are immense: enhanced concentration, reduced stress, and a calmer, more centered mind. Incorporate these techniques into your practice, experiment to see what works best for you, and watch as your ability to concentrate sharpens over time.

Remember, the journey to better focus is not about perfection; it's about consistent practice and compassionate self-awareness. Let's embrace this journey with an open heart and a focused mind.

Balancing Work and Mindfulness

In today's fast-paced world, it can seem almost impossible to balance the demands of work with the necessity of mindfulness. Many of us juggle deadlines, meetings, and a never-ending to-do list that often leaves us feeling overwhelmed and stressed. But what if integrating mindfulness into your workday could actually enhance your productivity and well-being? It's all about strategically weaving mindfulness practices into your daily routine to create a harmonious balance.

First, let's tackle the misconception that mindfulness takes up too much time. You don't need an hour-long meditation session to feel its benefits. Instead, try mini-meditations throughout your day. A simple 5-minute breathing exercise between meetings can clear your mind and improve focus. Another effective technique is the "STOP" method: Stop what you're doing, Take a breath, Observe your thoughts and feelings, and Proceed with intention. This quick practice can be a game-changer for regaining your center in a hectic workday.

But mindfulness doesn't have to be limited to these pauses. You can infuse it into your tasks. When answering emails, focus entirely on the message you're crafting. Turn off notifications so you can be present with each word and intention. At meetings, practice mindful listening. This means really hearing what others are saying without planning your next comment. Not only does this improve communication, but it also fosters a work environment where everyone feels heard and valued.

Another practical way to introduce mindfulness into work is by creating a mindful workspace. This doesn't mean you need to overhaul your office but making small adjustments can make a big difference. Declutter your desk to reduce distractions. Add elements that bring you peace, like a small plant or a photo that grounds you. A well-organized and pleasant workspace can significantly impact your mental state and productivity.

For those who work remotely, the lines between work and personal life can blur easily. Establishing boundaries is essential. Start your day with a morning ritual that sets your intention. This could be as simple as a 10-minute meditation, a mindful walk, or even journaling. These activities can anchor you, making it easier to transition into work mode with focus and clarity.

Then there's the concept of mindful breaks. It's tempting to skip breaks, thinking it's a way to get more done. But mindful breaks can actually boost efficiency. Stepping away from your desk for a short walk, stretching, or even a 5-minute meditation can rejuvenate your mind and body, making you more effective when you return to your tasks. Remember, these breaks are not just about resting; they are about resetting your mental state to maintain peak performance throughout the day.

Balancing work and mindfulness isn't just about individual practices—it's also about creating a workplace culture that values mental well-being. Encourage your team to take mindful breaks and lead by example. When scheduling meetings, try not to book them back-to-back. Allow some buffer time for everyone to regroup. And, if possible, incorporate mindfulness exercises into team meetings. Starting a meeting with a quick breathing exercise or a moment of silence can set a productive and focused tone.

Of course, we can't ignore technology. While it can be both a blessing and a curse, used mindfully, it can support your balance between work and mindfulness. There are numerous apps designed to help you integrate mindfulness practices into your daily routine. Some remind you to take breaks, others guide you through a quick meditation, and some even offer stress-relief exercises tailored to your needs.

As you become more adept at balancing work and mindfulness, you'll likely notice shifts not just in your work performance but in your overall well-being. Reduced stress levels, better focus, and a greater sense of peace are just a few of the benefits. Remember, the goal isn't to add another task to your already busy schedule; it's to seamlessly blend mindfulness into your existing routine to enhance your quality of life.

While consistent practice is key, be gentle with yourself. There will be days when it feels like you can't find a moment for mindfulness, and that's okay. The idea is to create an overall pattern of incorporating these practices rather than aiming for perfection. Some weeks might be more balanced than others, and learning to accept and adapt to that variability is part of the journey.

In conclusion, balancing work and mindfulness is a dynamic process that requires intentionality and adaptability. By starting small and gradually incorporating mindful practices into your daily routine, you can create a more harmonious work-life balance that fosters both professional success and personal well-being. It's about finding what works best for you and continuously adjusting as needed. Through mindfulness, you can transform the way you approach work and, ultimately, enhance your overall mental and emotional health.

Chapter 10: Emotional Regulation Through Mindfulness

Embracing mindfulness enables us to navigate our emotions with a calm and steady hand. By tuning into the present moment, we can recognize our feelings as they arise—whether they're joyful, sorrowful, or somewhere in between—without being swept away by them. This nuanced awareness allows us to respond thoughtfully rather than reacting impulsively. It's about cultivating a space between our emotions and actions, where we can choose our responses with intention and clarity. Imagine the freedom of being less dictated by mood swings and stress, and more guided by a composed, mindful presence. Through regular practice, mindfulness becomes a reliable anchor, steadying us amidst life's emotional storms and enhancing our overall mental well-being.

Recognizing Emotions

Emotional regulation is pivotal for anyone aiming to enhance their mental well-being, and recognizing your emotions is the first, crucial step in that journey. Emotions can feel like wild horses, dragging you in directions you never intended to go. Yet, by recognizing these emotions, you set the stage for a more mindful and controlled response. Instead of being a passenger on a rollercoaster, you become the one holding the reins.

It's about more than just identifying whether you're happy, sad, angry, or scared. It's digging deeper and understanding the nuances. Imagine feeling a pit in your stomach. Is it anxiety, guilt, or excitement? Each of these emotions feels similar physically but stems from different roots and leads to different actions. That's why recognizing emotions isn't just about labeling them; it's about understanding their origin and impact on your actions and thoughts.

Our brains are wired to recognize and process emotions, but we often don't give ourselves the time or space to do it properly. The hustle of daily life can turn emotions into background noise, creating stress and confusion. Mindfulness offers the tools to tune into this emotional frequency, turning noise into a clear signal.

Start by paying attention to physical cues. Emotional reactions often manifest physically before we're consciously aware of them. A clenched jaw could signify stress or anger. A tight chest might indicate anxiety or sadness. When these physical symptoms arise, take a moment to pause and ask yourself, "What am I feeling right now?"

Another effective technique is to name your emotions. Psychologists call this "affect labeling". When you name the emotion you're experiencing, you essentially put a boundary around it, making it less overwhelming. Statements like "I am feeling anxious" or "This is making me frustrated" help in taking an objective look at your emotional state.

Don't judge yourself for what you're feeling. Emotions are a natural part of human experience. They aren't good or bad—they just are. Judgment often leads to further emotional distress, complicating your ability to deal with what's actually happening. Instead, approach your emotions with curiosity. Ask yourself, "Why am I feeling this way?" rather than "Why on earth am I so mad?" It's a subtle shift, but it makes a world of difference.

Journaling can be immensely beneficial in recognizing and understanding emotions. By putting pen to paper, you allow your thoughts and feelings to flow freely, offering insights you might not have accessed otherwise. It's like having a conversation with yourself, providing clarity and perspective.

Another tool in your kit could be mindfulness meditation. Practices like the body scan or breath awareness help in grounding you in the present moment. Once you are present, it becomes easier to notice the emotions swirling within. For example, during a body scan, you might notice tension in your shoulders.

Instead of merely noting it and moving on, delve deeper—what is causing this tension? Perhaps it's a worry about an upcoming meeting or lingering stress from a past conversation.

As you hone the skill of recognizing your emotions, you'll find it easier to respond mindfully rather than react impulsively. Picture this: Instead of snapping at a loved one when you're irritated, you recognize the irritation, understand its source, and choose a more measured response. The transformation might seem small but has profound effects on your relationships and overall peace.

It's also worth mentioning the role of compassion—both for yourself and others. When you recognize your own emotions, you become attuned to the emotions of others, fostering empathy and understanding. This doesn't mean you have to solve everyone's problems, but a simple acknowledgment of their feelings can work wonders. Sometimes, saying "I see that you're upset, and it's okay to feel that way" can be incredibly validating for another person.

Moreover, recognizing emotions can serve as a guide to your actions. Your emotional responses give clues about what you value and what you might need to change. If a particular situation consistently makes you anxious, it might be worth exploring why and considering adjustments to minimize that stressor.

One caution: Be wary of over-analysis. While it's important to recognize and explore your emotions, getting trapped in a cycle of overthinking can be counterproductive. Sometimes, a feeling is just a feeling, and that's okay. It's about finding balance—acknowledge, understand, and then move forward.

Recognizing emotions is like learning a new language. Initially, it can be challenging, and you might feel awkward or frustrated. However, with consistent practice, it becomes second nature. You start to notice patterns and triggers, enabling you to act with insight and intention rather than being at the mercy of fluctuating feelings.

Incorporating these practices into your daily routine doesn't have to be time-consuming. Micro-moments, like a mindful breath before responding to an email or a quick check-in during your commute, can make significant differences. The goal isn't to become an emotionless being but to cultivate a sense of awareness and control over your emotional landscape.

In our fast-paced world, taking time to recognize and understand your emotions might seem like a luxury. Yet, it's essential for deeper mindfulness and emotional regulation. These skills contribute directly to reduced stress and greater mental well-being. So, take a moment now and then to pause, observe, and reflect. Your emotional health will thank you for it.

Mindful Responses

Let's consider the concept of mindful responses. In the hustle and bustle of daily life, it's easy to react impulsively to situations that trigger emotional responses. Whether it's a terse email from a colleague or an unexpected traffic jam, these moments can often lead us to react in ways that we later regret. Mindfulness, however, offers a buffer—a pause between stimulus and response that allows us to choose our actions more wisely.

When we talk about mindful responses, we're referring to that magical space where choice exists. Viktor Frankl, a renowned psychiatrist and Holocaust survivor, once said, "Between stimulus and response there is a space. In that space is our power to choose our response. In our response lies our growth and our freedom." By cultivating mindfulness, we expand this space, enabling ourselves to respond in ways that align with our values and long-term goals.

Imagine being able to respond to life's challenges with a calm, centered approach, rather than in a reactive, knee-jerk manner. This doesn't mean suppressing your emotions or pretending everything is perfect. It means recognizing your feelings, understanding their origins, and then choosing a response that serves you and others well. Let's dive deeper into how we can practice this in our everyday lives.

First, it's essential to develop an awareness of your emotional triggers. You can't change what you're not aware of. Begin by observing your thoughts and emotions throughout the day. Mindfulness meditation practices like body scans and mindful breathing can help you tune into your internal states. Are you feeling anxious before a big meeting? Do you notice anger welling up when someone cuts you off in traffic? Naming these emotions can diffuse their power and provide a moment of clarity.

Next, practice the art of the pause. When you feel an emotional surge, take a deep breath. Inhale slowly and exhale completely. This simple act can prevent you from reacting blindly. In that brief moment of pausing, you create space for a mindful response. It's not about controlling the situation but about controlling your reaction to it. This gap gives you the chance to evaluate your options and choose a response that aligns with your inner values.

One of the most powerful ways to develop mindful responses is through regular meditation practice. This doesn't mean you need to spend hours sitting in silence. Even a few minutes a day can make a significant difference. Meditation helps train your mind to recognize thoughts and emotions without becoming overwhelmed by them. Over time, you build the mental muscles needed to stay grounded and respond thoughtfully even in stressful situations.

Let's talk about the importance of self-compassion in this journey. Everyone has moments when they react poorly. When this happens, it's crucial to approach yourself with kindness rather than self-criticism. Acknowledge that you're a work in progress. Reflect on what you can learn from the situation and how you might respond differently in the future. This gentle, forgiving perspective fosters resilience and encourages continued growth.

Another key aspect is practicing empathy—not just towards others, but also towards oneself. When you find yourself reacting strongly, ask yourself why this particular situation is evoking such intense emotions. Are there past experiences influencing your current reaction? Understanding the deeper layers of your emotions can lead to more compassionate and mindful responses

Developing mindful responses also involves setting boundaries and being clear about your needs. For instance, if you receive a critical email, instead of firing back immediately, pause and consider your best course of action. Would it be more productive to request a meeting to discuss the issue in person? By responding mindfully, you create a more constructive and compassionate environment for communication.

Creating a supportive environment can also significantly help in cultivating mindful responses. Surround yourself with people who practice mindfulness and emotional regulation. Engage in open conversations about your experiences and challenges. Sharing your journey with others creates a sense of community and accountability, making it easier to stay committed to your practice.

Mindfulness extends beyond individual responses. It's an approach to life that influences how we interact with the world around us. When you cultivate mindful responses, you contribute to a more harmonious and peaceful world. Each mindful response sets a ripple effect, encouraging others to respond in kind.

Incorporating mindful responses into your daily life doesn't mean you need to be perfect. It's about progress, not perfection. Start with small, manageable steps. Pay attention to your breath before responding to a difficult question. Take a moment to consider your words before engaging in a heated discussion. Small changes, when consistently practiced, lead to significant transformation over time.

So, as you go about your day, remember that you have the power to choose your response in every situation. This power, when harnessed through mindfulness, can transform your interactions and improve your overall well-being. Start today by taking a few mindful breaths, and notice how this simple practice can create a ripple effect of positive change in your life.

Chapter 11: Meditation for Better Sleep

When it comes to achieving a restful night, meditation is a game-changer. Evening meditation practices can help you wind down and disconnect from the rush of daily life, easing your mind into a peaceful state that's conducive to sleep. Imagine letting go of the day's stress, balancing breathing, and focusing on calming thoughts—this simple routine can make a world of difference. Guided sleep meditations are especially effective, as they gently lead you through steps that relax both body and mind. By integrating these practices into your nightly routine, you create a sanctuary for rest, fostering rejuvenating sleep that sets a positive tone for each day.

Evening Meditation Practices

As the day winds down, the quest for a serene and restful night begins. Evening meditation practices can serve as a gentle bridge from the busyness of daily life to the tranquility of sleep. Let's dive into some transformational methods to make your evenings more peaceful and your sleep more restorative.

First, let's appreciate the backdrop of an evening meditation. The sun has set, the environment is quieter, and there's a natural inclination to become more introspective. Leveraging this calm energy can significantly enhance the effectiveness of your practice. Start by creating a consistent evening ritual. Much like a morning routine sets the tone for the day, an evening ritual can cultivate the mental and physical conditions conducive to a restful sleep.

Consider starting your meditation an hour before bedtime. This buffer allows you to disentangle from any lingering thoughts of the day. One straightforward yet powerful technique is **progressive relaxation**. Begin by finding a comfortable position, either sitting or lying down. Close your eyes and take a few deep breaths. Visualize each part of your body, starting from your toes and working your way up to your head, slowly releasing tension as you go. This method not only calms the mind but also prepares the body for the deep relaxation needed for sleep.

To deepen your practice, sound can be a remarkably impactful aid. Consider adding some soft, ambient music or nature sounds like rain or ocean waves. These auditory cues signal to your brain that it's time to unwind and relax. Another potent tool is guided sleep meditations. These usually combine deep breathing exercises with soothing narratives that help shift your mind's focus from active thoughts to a more restful state.

An effective meditation technique that can transform your evenings is **mindful reflection**. Set aside a few moments to reflect on your day, focusing specifically on gratitude. What were three things that went well today? What small victories or moments of joy did you experience? Reflecting on these aspects can nurture a positive mindset, replacing stress or anxiety with feelings of contentment and peace, making it easier to drift off to sleep.

Breathwork is another cornerstone of evening meditation practices. Simple techniques like *4-7-8 breathing* can be incredibly soothing. Inhale quietly through your nose for a count of four, hold your breath for seven, and exhale completely through your mouth for a count of eight. Repeat this cycle a few times. This breathing technique helps to calm the nervous system and prepare your body for sleep.

Moving from thoughts to the breath creates a powerful shift. However, staying present can sometimes be challenging, especially if the mind is cluttered with unfinished tasks or unresolved worries. Here, incorporating visualization can make a significant difference. Picture a tranquil scene: a quiet beach, a serene forest, or even floating on a soft cloud. Let these calming images replace the busy chatter of your day, drawing you into a state of deep relaxation.

Creating an optimal physical environment also plays a crucial role. Dim the lights and set a comfortable room temperature to signal to your brain that it's time to relax. Incorporate calming scents like lavender or chamomile through essential oils or scented candles. The sense of smell can directly influence the brain's pathways related to relaxation and stress, helping you to slip into a calmer state more effortlessly.

Being consistent with your practice is key. Just like any other habit, the benefits of evening meditation compound with regular practice. Try to meditate at the same time and in the same spot each evening. Over time, your body and mind will start to associate this routine with the onset of rest, making the transition to sleep smoother and more natural.

If you find that thoughts keep intruding, don't get frustrated. It's perfectly natural. Instead, acknowledge each thought and gently guide your focus back to your breath or your chosen visualization. This non-judgmental approach helps in cultivating patience and kindness towards oneself, essential qualities for a more profound meditation experience.

Mindful journaling can also complement your evening meditation. Spend five to ten minutes writing down any persistent thoughts, worries, or tasks. This act of "downloading" your brain can free up mental space, making it easier to relax and engage fully in your meditation practice. Plus, it provides a tangible record that you can refer back to, helping you track patterns and progress over time.

On nights when settling down feels particularly challenging, don't hesitate to adapt your techniques. Maybe sitting up feels too energizing—then lie down. Or perhaps focusing on your breath seems too hard—try focusing on a mantra or an affirmation instead. The goal is to make the practice work for you, not the other way around.

When integrated into your evening routine, these meditation practices can pave the way for a better night's sleep. You'll find that the more you practice, the more naturally restful sleep becomes. Evening meditation is not just about addressing sleep issues but cultivating a sense of peace that extends into all corners of your life. So, take these moments of tranquility and transform your nights into a sanctuary of calm.

Guided Sleep Meditations

In the hustle and bustle of our day-to-day lives, a good night's sleep can sometimes feel like an elusive dream. Stress, overthinking, and the constant bombardment of stimuli from our environment often lead to sleepless nights and restless hours. Enter guided sleep meditations—a profoundly effective method designed to calm the mind, relax the body, and invite restful, restorative sleep.

Guided sleep meditations are carefully structured audio or verbal narratives that guide you through a series of calming thoughts, visualizations, and breathing exercises. These meditations don't just help you fall asleep; they create a receptive state that primes your body and mind for deeper, more holistic relaxation.

Let's talk about visualizations first. One of the most effective techniques involves visualizing a serene environment, such as a quiet beach, a peaceful meadow, or a cozy, warm room with a crackling fireplace. Imagine the soft sounds, the ambient smells, and the comforting visuals. With each breath, let yourself sink deeper into this mindful escape.

This sort of mental imagery works wonders because it leverages the brain's ability to create reality from perception. When you vividly imagine a tranquil scene, your physical body reacts as though you are actually there. Your heart rate slows, your blood pressure drops, and your muscles start to relax. Essentially, your mind paves the way for your body to follow.

Breathing exercises are another cornerstone of guided sleep meditations. Techniques like the 4-7-8 method can be particularly effective. Here, you inhale for four seconds, hold the breath for seven seconds, and then exhale slowly for eight seconds. This deliberate pattern not only shifts your focus away from intrusive thoughts but also engages the body's parasympathetic nervous system, making relaxation almost inevitable.

If you're new to guided sleep meditations, starting with a simple body scan meditation can be incredibly beneficial. This type of meditation encourages you to bring awareness to different parts of your body, beginning from the head and moving gradually down to the toes. As you focus on each area, you're encouraged to release tension and breathe deeply, allowing each part of your body to become progressively more relaxed.

Many guided sleep meditations also incorporate elements of progressive muscle relaxation. This technique involves tensing and then slowly releasing various muscle groups. By doing so, you not only help release physical tension but also become more aware of where you hold stress in your body. The key is to pay attention to the subtle changes you feel as tension melts away.

Let's not forget the power of a soothing voice. Listening to a calm, steady voice guiding you through these steps can be highly effective. The tone, pace, and rhythm of the guide's voice help synchronize your mind's tempo with a slower, more relaxed state. It's like having a gentle beacon guiding you into the safe harbor of sleep.

Some guided sleep meditations also incorporate background music or ambient sounds, such as ocean waves, gentle rain, or soft instrumental music. The right auditory environment can make a significant difference, creating a soothing backdrop that further encourages relaxation and helps drown out disruptive noises.

Many people find the combination of voice and music an optimal way to create a meditative state conducive to sleep. These auditory elements work together, allowing the mind to let go of stress and prepare for sleep, much like a well-orchestrated symphony. The beauty of this approach is that it doesn't require any prior meditation experience. You simply need to lie down, listen, and follow along.

While the immediate benefit of guided sleep meditation is, of course, better sleep, regular practice offers long-term advantages. Over time, you'll notice that you fall asleep faster and experience more restful sleep without the constant interruption of waking thoughts. Your overall mental well-being and daily energy levels can see a remarkable improvement.

Ultimately, the beauty of guided sleep meditations lies in their accessibility and adaptability. There's no one-size-fits-all approach, so feel free to experiment with different types, durations, and themes until you find what works best for you. It's your journey to a better night's sleep, and guided sleep meditation can be a faithful companion along the way.

Integrating guided sleep meditations into your nightly routine doesn't have to be complicated. You could start by setting aside 10 to 15 minutes before going to bed to listen to a meditation. Make sure your sleeping environment is comfortable, and eliminate any distractions like bright lights or electronic noise.

Many people find it helpful to use meditation apps or online platforms that offer a variety of guided sleep meditations. These resources often allow you to choose from different themes, lengths, and styles so you can tailor your practice to what you need on any given night. Explore options like Headspace, Calm, or Insight Timer to get started.

If technology isn't your cup of tea, you can also record your own guided sleep meditation. Use your voice or someone else's, reading a script of calming phrases, visualizations, and breathing instructions. This personalized approach ensures that every element, from the tone to the pacing, is precisely what you find most relaxing.

Another useful tip: consistency is key. Try to make guided sleep meditation a regular part of your bedtime routine. The more you practice, the easier it will become to reach that desired state of relaxation. It's much like training a muscle—repetition strengthens the pathway.

Don't be discouraged if you don't notice immediate results. Like any form of meditation, guided sleep meditations require a bit of patience and practice. Over time, you'll likely find that your transition from wakefulness to sleep becomes smoother and more natural.

In essence, guided sleep meditations offer a simple yet profoundly effective way to improve your sleep quality. By calming the mind and relaxing the body, they provide a holistic approach to achieving restful, restorative sleep—an essential component of overall mental well-being.

Chapter 12: Mindfulness and Relationships

Mindfulness can be a game-changer in our relationships, providing a foundation for healthier, deeper connections with the people we care about. By practicing mindfulness, we create space to truly listen and understand others, improving our communication and fostering empathy. It's not just about being present in conversations, but about bringing a genuine sense of awareness to all our interactions. This heightened awareness helps us recognize and manage our own emotions better, allowing us to respond rather than react, which leads to more constructive and compassionate exchanges. With mindfulness, we're better equipped to navigate the complexities of human relationships, embracing both the joy and the challenges with grace and resilience.

Improving Communication

Effective communication is foundational to any healthy relationship, whether it's with a partner, a friend, a family member, or even a co-worker. Often, our conversations can become mired in misunderstandings, misinterpretations, and emotional triggers. This is where mindfulness steps in, offering us a powerful toolkit to navigate these challenges.

When we talk about improving communication through mindfulness, it's not just about paying attention to the words we say. It's a holistic approach that involves being fully present in the moment, listening actively, and responding thoughtfully. Imagine a heated discussion. With mindfulness, instead of reacting impulsively, you pause, take a deep breath, and observe your emotional state. This small act of mindfulness can completely shift the dynamic of the conversation.

Listening is an art, and mindfulness can transform us into better listeners. Usually, when someone else is speaking, our minds are busy formulating responses or judgments. True mindful listening, however, requires us to silence that inner chatter and focus entirely on the speaker. This doesn't just mean hearing their words, but also picking up on non-verbal cues like body language and facial expressions. Over time, this practice nurtures greater empathy and understanding.

One technique to foster mindful communication is the "pause and reflect" method. Before speaking, take a brief moment to consider your words. Are they necessary? Are they kind? Are they true? This not only helps in avoiding hurtful comments but also promotes clarity and honesty in your exchanges.

Another aspect of mindful communication is maintaining eye contact. It may sound simple, but in a world inundated with digital distractions, eye contact can be rare. Maintaining eye contact signifies that you value the other person and are genuinely engaged. This simple gesture can make conversations more meaningful and intimate.

Non-violent communication (NVC) is a powerful framework that aligns closely with mindfulness principles. Developed by Marshall Rosenberg, NVC emphasizes expressing oneself honestly while also being empathetic towards others. It involves four key components: observations, feelings, needs, and requests. By focusing on these elements, you can communicate in a way that fosters connection and mutual understanding.

Let's not forget the importance of body awareness in mindful communication. How often do we find ourselves clenching our fists or grinding our teeth during disagreements? By tuning into these physical sensations, we can become more aware of our stress responses. This awareness provides a golden opportunity to ease tension and approach the conversation more calmly.

Moreover, mindfulness teaches us to embrace silence. In many cultures, silence in conversation is often perceived as awkward or uncomfortable. However, moments of silence can actually provide space for deeper reflection and more thoughtful responses. It's during these pauses that genuine understanding often emerges.

Conflict is inevitable in any relationship, but how we handle it can make all the difference. Mindfulness can equip us with the skills to manage conflict more constructively. Instead of jumping to defensiveness, we learn to acknowledge the other person's perspective. By practicing non-attachment to our viewpoints, we become more open to compromise and solutions that benefit all parties involved.

Regular mindfulness practice also enhances our emotional intelligence, which is critical for effective communication. Emotional intelligence involves recognizing, understanding, and managing our own emotions, while also being sensitive to the emotions of others. Through mindfulness, we develop a heightened awareness of our emotional triggers and learn to navigate them with greater ease and grace.

It's worth mentioning that communication isn't solely about speaking and listening. Written communication, especially in today's digital age, is just as crucial. Whether it's an email, a text message, or a social media post, mindfulness can help us communicate more effectively in writing. Taking a moment to read over what we've written before hitting send can prevent misunderstandings and ensure our message is clear and considerate.

Mindful communication also extends to self-talk, the way we communicate with ourselves. Often, we can be our harshest critics, engaging in negative self-talk that erodes our confidence and well-being. By bringing mindfulness into our internal dialogue, we can cultivate a more compassionate and supportive relationship with ourselves.

Incorporating mindfulness into communication doesn't happen overnight. It's a gradual process that involves continuous practice and self-reflection. But the benefits are manifold: deeper connections, fewer misunderstandings, and a more harmonious relational dynamic. So, the next time you find yourself in conversation, take a moment to breathe, be present, and communicate mindfully.

Fostering Empathy

Imagine a world where empathy is the cornerstone of daily interactions. People meeting each other with genuine care and understanding, regardless of their differences, creates a community that thrives on mutual respect and compassion. This might seem idealistic, but mindfulness offers us a pragmatic route toward achieving this. By tuning into our own emotions and the feelings of others, we can foster a deeper sense of empathy that enriches our relationships.

The journey of nurturing empathy begins with self-awareness. When we're mindful, we're more aware of our thoughts, emotions, and physical sensations in real-time. This heightened self-awareness allows us to recognize how our own emotional states influence our behavior and interactions. Understanding our own emotional landscape is the first step to empathizing with others. It's about moving from a reflexive reaction to a thoughtful response, where we consider not just our own feelings but also the emotions and perspectives of those around us.

Practicing mindfulness encourages us to slow down and consider our reactions before we express them. It invites us to listen deeply to others, not just with our ears but with our entire being. This form of deep listening can be transformative in relationships. Rather than preparing our next argument or zoning out, we are fully present with the person speaking. We hear not just the words, but the emotions and intentions behind them. This creates a space where genuine understanding can flourish.

One powerful mindfulness exercise for fostering empathy is the "Loving-Kindness Meditation." In this practice, you silently repeat phrases aimed at generating goodwill towards yourself and others. Phrases such as "May I be happy," "May I be healthy," and "May I live with ease" are extended to others, starting with those close to us and gradually including all beings. This meditation cultivates a sense of universal compassion, encouraging us to see the inherent value in everyone, even those we find challenging.

Another aspect of mindfulness that fosters empathy is non-judgmental awareness. Often, we categorize people based on our experiences and biases, which can blind us to their true selves. By adopting a mindset of acceptance and curiosity, we approach each person as they are in the present moment, suspending our preconceived notions and judgments. This openness facilitates deeper connections and allows us to appreciate the unique experiences that shape each individual.

Mindfulness also helps in managing our emotional triggers. We all have situations or individuals that provoke strong reactions in us. By practicing mindfulness, we learn to observe these triggers without immediately getting swept away by them. We can acknowledge our feelings, take a step back, and choose a more compassionate response. This ability to regulate our emotions is crucial in fostering empathy, as it enables us to respond with kindness rather than defensiveness or aggression.

Incorporating mindfulness into our daily routines doesn't require grand gestures. Simple practices can have profound effects on our capacity for empathy. Begin with mindful breathing. Take a few moments each day to focus on your breath, noticing the sensation of the air entering and leaving your body. This practice anchors you in the present moment and calms the mind, creating a fertile ground for empathy to grow.

Mindfulness walks can also be an enriching practice. As you walk, pay attention to your surroundings, the sensations in your body, and the rhythm of your steps. This practice helps ground you in the present, making you more receptive to the world and the people around you. When we're fully present, we are more attuned to the emotions of others, enhancing our ability to empathize.

For those looking to deepen their mindfulness and empathy practice, journaling can be a powerful tool. At the end of each day, take a few moments to reflect on your interactions. Write about moments where you felt connected and those where you struggled to empathize. This reflection helps you become more aware of your emotional patterns and provides insights into how you can cultivate a more empathetic approach in future interactions.

Empathy also involves setting healthy boundaries. It might seem counterintuitive, but being mindful of our own needs and limits is essential for sustaining empathy. By ensuring that we are not overwhelmed or depleted, we can be more genuinely present and compassionate with others. Boundaries are not walls but guidelines that help maintain the balance between self-care and caring for others.

Mindfulness and compassion are mutually reinforcing. As we practice mindfulness, we naturally become more compassionate towards ourselves and others. Likewise, a compassionate mindset enhances our mindfulness practice. It's a virtuous cycle that not only fosters empathy but also promotes overall mental well-being. In this way, mindfulness serves as both the path and the destination in our journey toward empathetic relationships.

Finally, remember that fostering empathy through mindfulness is a continuous journey. It requires patience, persistence, and kindness towards ourselves. There will be moments of frustration and setbacks, but each step taken with mindfulness brings us closer to a more empathetic world. By committing to this practice, we can transform our relationships, our communities, and ultimately, ourselves.

In conclusion, fostering empathy through mindfulness is one of the most impactful ways to enhance our relationships and create a more compassionate world. By practicing self-awareness, deep listening, loving-kindness meditation, and non-judgmental awareness, we can cultivate a deeper sense of empathy. Incorporating simple mindfulness practices into our daily lives and reflecting on our interactions can make a profound difference. Together, these practices help build a foundation of empathy that enriches our interactions and promotes greater mental well-being for ourselves and those around us.

Chapter 13: The Role of Breath in Meditation

B reath is more than just a conduit for oxygen; it's a profound anchor for the wandering mind in meditation. When we center our attention on each inhale and exhale, we create a gateway to the present moment, reducing stress and increasing clarity. It's almost magical how something as simple as our breath can ground us, bringing a wave of calm and focus. Consider it both a tool and a teacher—a constant reminder that in the hustle and bustle of life, peace is just a breath away. Embracing this practice not only deepens our meditation but also equips us with a natural way to navigate life's ups and downs with grace and poise.

Breath Awareness Techniques

When diving into the realm of meditation, one of the most fundamental elements we often overlook is our breath. Simple yet profound, breath awareness is a core technique that can transform your meditation practice from a mundane ritual to a deeply enlightening experience. Imagine unwinding a tangled ball of yarn; that's what breath awareness does for your mind. It unravels the knots of stress, anxiety, and distraction—one breath at a time.

Before delving into the specifics of breath awareness techniques, it's essential to understand why breath holds such power. Breath can be both a voluntary and involuntary action, connecting the conscious and unconscious. This dual nature makes it a bridge between the mind and body, grounding you in the present moment effortlessly and efficiently.

Let's start with a simple technique called mindful breathing. Sit in a comfortable position and gently close your eyes. Focus on your breath as it enters and exits through your nose. Feel the cool air entering, the subtle warmth as you exhale. You don't need to change your breath; instead, just become an observer of its natural rhythm. This technique isn't about controlling the breath but about noticing it. Doing this for even a few minutes can have a surprising impact on your mental state—calming, centering, and grounding you.

Another effective method is the 4-7-8 technique, popularized by Dr. Andrew Weil. Here, you inhale through your nose for four seconds, hold the breath for seven seconds, and exhale slowly through your mouth for eight seconds. This technique is particularly useful for those who find it hard to shut their mind off at the end of a busy day. It engages the parasympathetic nervous system—the rest and digest function of our body—guiding you into a state of deep relaxation.

For those struggling with focus during meditation, the counting breath technique can be a game-changer. Sit comfortably and close your eyes. Begin by counting "one" as you inhale and "two" as you exhale. Continue counting up to ten and then start over. Counting the breaths can serve as an anchor, preventing your mind from wandering off. If you lose count, don't worry— just gently bring your attention back to the breath and start again. This technique strengthens your concentration muscle, making it easier to stay present during other meditation practices.

Visualization can also be a valuable tool. Picture your breath as a wave that travels up and down your body. As you inhale, visualize the wave starting from your toes, rising to the top of your head. As you exhale, imagine it flowing back down to your toes. This adds an element of mindfulness, enhancing the tactile and sensory experience of breathing. It's as if your breath becomes a brush, painting calm across the canvas of your body.

While the previous techniques are relatively simple, there are more nuanced methods for those looking to deepen their practice. Techniques like alternate nostril breathing or Nadi Shodhana work on a more subtle level, balancing the two hemispheres of the brain and promoting emotional stability. To practice this, sit comfortably and use your right thumb to close your right nostril. Inhale through your left nostril, then close your left nostril with your right ring finger, and exhale through your right nostril. Repeat in reverse, and continue this alternating pattern. It's a bit more advanced but can significantly elevate your mindfulness game.

Then there's the technique of breath retention, or Kumbhaka. This involves pausing at the top of the inhale and the bottom of the exhale, holding your breath for varying lengths of time. Beginners should start slow, holding for just a couple of seconds, before gradually extending the duration. The practice of breath retention is believed to enhance mental clarity and dissolve accumulated stress. However, it should be approached with caution and ideally taught by a qualified instructor to avoid hyperventilation or dizziness.

Incorporating breath awareness into daily life extends beyond the meditation cushion. Try practicing mindful breaths while waiting at a red light, standing in line at the grocery store, or even during work breaks. The essence of mindfulness lies in integrating these practices into daily life seamlessly, making the ordinary extraordinary. These techniques remind us that we always have a tool at our disposal to bring us back to the present moment, to ground ourselves amidst chaos.

As you progress, it's important to remember that mastery comes through consistent practice. It's not about achieving perfection but about fostering a state of awareness and acceptance. Every time you bring your attention back to your breath, you're reinforcing a habit of mindfulness. This incremental progress may seem small but over time, it builds a resilient mind capable of facing life's challenges with calm and clarity.

Whether you're a beginner or someone looking to deepen your practice, integrating these breath awareness techniques can provide you with a sturdy foundation for mindfulness and meditation. Think of your breath as an untapped resource, always available, yet often overlooked. By tapping into its potential, you can navigate through the ebb and flow of life with more grace, focus, and peace.

So, take a deep breath. Feel it fully, and let yourself be present in this moment. This simple act has the power to transform your inner world, one breath at a time.

Pranayama Exercises

Breath is more than just a vital function for survival; it's a bridge to a serene mind and a centered soul. Pranayama, the ancient practice of breath control, offers various techniques that can lead to profound states of mindfulness and a deeper meditation practice. They provide an excellent way to synchronize the body, mind, and spirit, creating a harmony that resonates well beyond the meditation cushion.

Incorporating pranayama exercises into your routine can bring immediate benefits. Think of it as tuning an instrument before you play; it ensures that everything is in harmony. Even if you're new to pranayama, there's no need to feel intimidated. Start simple and gradually build up your practice. The beauty of pranayama is that it can be adapted to fit your life and comfort level.

Let's begin with one of the most accessible techniques: Nadi Shodhana, or alternate nostril breathing. This exercise helps clear the channels of the mind and balance the energy within your body. To practice, sit comfortably with your spine straight. Use your right thumb to close your right nostril and inhale deeply through the left. Next, close the left nostril with your ring finger and exhale through the right nostril. Continue this alternating pattern, always inhaling through one nostril and exhaling through the other. Feel the calm wash over you as you bring your mind to focus on each breath.

You might notice how your mind starts to wander initially. That's perfectly okay. Gently bring your focus back to your breath without judgment. With time and practice, the periods of focus and clarity will extend. And remember, the aim is not perfection but progress.

Another powerful pranayama technique is Kapalabhati, or skull-shining breath. This is a bit more vigorous and energizing. Seating yourself comfortably, take a deep breath in, and then begin short, forceful exhalations using your abdominal muscles. Allow the inhalation to happen passively between each exhalation. Start with a cycle of 30 breaths, pause, and notice how your body feels. Your mind may suddenly feel like a clear, polished window letting in the light.

Kapalabhati is particularly useful when you need a quick boost of energy or when you feel sluggish. It's like pressing the reset button on your mental state, clearing away mental cobwebs and allowing fresh, new thoughts to flow in. It is, however, more physically demanding, so those with respiratory issues or high blood pressure should consult with a healthcare provider before trying it.

If you're seeking relaxation and stress relief, the Ujjayi breath, often called ocean breath, is your go-to. This technique involves breathing in and out through the nose with a slight constriction at the back of the throat, producing a sound reminiscent of ocean waves. The slow, rhythmic nature of Ujjayi breath helps soothe the nervous system and brings a deep sense of calm.

To practice Ujjayi breath, sit comfortably, close your eyes, and take a deep breath through your nose. As you exhale, gently constrict the muscles at the back of your throat, creating a soft whispering sound, like the sound of the sea. Continue this breath for several minutes, allowing yourself to sink deeper into relaxation with each breath.

Next up, Bhramari, or the humming bee breath, serves as an excellent tool for calming the mind and reducing anxiety. To perform Bhramari, sit in a comfortable position and close your eyes. Take a deep inhalation and, as you exhale, make a humming sound like a bee. Focus on the vibrations within your body and let them resonate through your entire being.

Bhramari is particularly effective before sleep or during periods of high stress. The gentle vibrations create a sense of grounding and tranquility, pulling you back to a state of balance. Over time, you may notice it becomes easier to manage stress and anxiety in your daily life.

Amongst the varying techniques, Sitali breath, also known as cooling breath, provides a refreshing break. This exercise can be particularly helpful in calming the mind and body after a stressful day. To practice Sitali breath, sit comfortably and curl your tongue to form a tube, then inhale through this tube. If curling your tongue isn't possible, you can simply purse your lips and inhale through your mouth. After inhaling, close your mouth and exhale through your nose. A few minutes of Sitali breath can leave you feeling cooler and more relaxed.

The regular practice of these pranayama techniques can bring about substantial changes in your mind and body. They help regulate the nervous system, reduce stress, and improve overall mental health. With time, these breathing exercises can deepen your meditation practice and enhance your sense of well-being. But remember, consistency is key. Dedicate a few minutes each day to pranayama, and you'll soon notice how it transforms your approach to life and meditation.

As you explore pranayama exercises, it's crucial to listen to your body. Breath control should never cause discomfort or strain. If you ever feel lightheaded or uneasy, stop and take a few moments to breathe normally. Pranayama is meant to be a gentle guiding force, not a rigorous activity.

In conclusion, pranayama offers a gateway to a richer, more fulfilling meditation practice. Through techniques like Nadi Shodhana, Kapalabhati, Ujjayi, Bhramari, and Sitali, you can find a method that resonates with your current needs and lifestyle. These exercises create a solid foundation for mindfulness, building resilience, balance, and peace from the inside out. Breathe deeply, and let your journey unfold naturally.

Chapter 14: Introducing Children to Mindfulness

As parents or caregivers, we all want to nurture children's emotional and mental well-being, and introducing them to mindfulness can be a transformative tool in their growth. It's not just about teaching kids to sit still; it's about equipping them with skills to navigate emotions and manage stress, right from a young age. Imagine the benefits of mindfulness practices embedded into their daily routines: improved focus, enhanced emotional regulation, and even better sleep patterns. Start with simple techniques that feel more like playful activities than formal exercises. When mindfulness becomes a family affair, it can foster stronger bonds and mutual emotional support, creating a shared journey towards mental wellness. By making mindfulness a natural part of life, children can carry these valuable habits into adulthood, ultimately enhancing their overall well-being in a fast-paced, ever-changing world.

Simple Techniques for Kids

Introducing mindfulness to kids can be a life-changing gift, helping them develop emotional intelligence, focus, and a sense of inner calm. But how do you make mindfulness accessible and engaging for young minds? The key is to keep it simple, playful, and fun. Here are some effective techniques to get started.

One of the simplest ways to teach kids mindfulness is through breathing exercises. "Take Five" is a popular method. Have your child stretch out one hand like a star. Then, with the index finger of their other hand, they trace the outline of their stretched hand, breathing in as they trace up and breathing out as they trace down. This combines tactile sensation with breath awareness, keeping their attention anchored in the present moment.

Another great technique is the "Mind Jar." Fill a clear jar with water, add glitter glue, and a bit of glitter. Shake it up and explain to the child that the swirling glitter represents their thoughts when they're anxious or upset. Watching the glitter settle to the bottom of the jar can help them understand how taking a moment to be still can help settle their minds. It's a visual and interactive way to understand the calming effects of mindfulness.

Consider incorporating "body scans" into their daily routine. This doesn't need to be as formal as adult practices. Have them lie down or sit comfortably and guide them through noticing different parts of their body, starting from their toes and moving to their head. Encourage them to pay attention to any sensations they might feel. This helps them develop a connection with their body and recognize how stress and emotions can manifest physically.

Make storytelling a part of their mindfulness practice. You can introduce stories that integrate mindfulness themes. Characters overcoming challenges by being present, taking deep breaths, or noticing their surroundings can make the concept relatable. After the story, engage them in a conversation about how the characters used mindfulness and how they can use similar techniques in their own lives.

If your child enjoys being active, "Mindful Walking" could be a great fit. Take them on a short walk and encourage them to notice their surroundings with all their senses. What do they hear? How does the ground feel under their feet? Can they smell any flowers or fresh air? This practice helps them understand that mindfulness isn't just about sitting still but can be integrated into everyday activities.

Creating a "Gratitude Tree" can also foster mindfulness. Each day, encourage your child to write down or draw something they're grateful for on a leaf-shaped piece of paper and add it to the "tree." This can be a poster on the wall or an actual small tree. Over time, they'll have a visual reminder of all the things they appreciate, cultivating a positive and mindful mindset.

Introducing guided imagery can also be an effective way. Lead them through a simple guided imagery exercise, like imagining a balloon they're holding. As they breathe in, the balloon fills up, and as they breathe out, they let it go and watch it fly away. This exercise visually connects the breath to a calming outcome, making it easier for them to grasp the benefits of deep, controlled breathing.

For younger kids, using stuffed animals can make mindfulness practice relatable. Have them lie down and place a stuffed animal on their belly. Ask them to watch how it rises and falls with each breath. This simple exercise can teach them about deep breathing in a fun and engaging way.

Incorporating mindfulness into their regular playtime can also work wonders. Use building blocks or puzzles as a way to practice focused attention. Encourage them to notice the colors, shapes, and how the pieces fit together. This practice helps in building their concentration muscles in a natural and playful way.

Introducing "Mindful Eating" can be a fun and eye-opening practice. During snack time, encourage them to eat slowly and notice the flavors, textures, and smells of their food. This can turn everyday routines into moments of mindfulness. It's a way to bring their attention fully to the present moment and appreciate it with all their senses.

Consider incorporating a "Feelings Wheel" into your daily routine. Create a simple wheel with different emotions like happy, sad, angry, and calm. At different times throughout the day, ask your child to point to how they're feeling. This can help them become more aware of their emotions and understand that it's okay to feel different things at different times.

Lastly, don't forget the power of music and dance. Put on some calming music and encourage your child to move in a way that feels good to them. This helps them connect with their body and express themselves. It can also be a gentle way to release any built-up stress or energy.

Always remember that the goal is not to force anything but to introduce mindfulness in a way that resonates with your child. Be patient and flexible, and make sure the practices are enjoyable. Your enthusiasm and consistency will set a positive example, paving the way for a more mindful and balanced life for your child.

Building a Family Practice

Introducing children to mindfulness is like planting seeds that will one day grow into resilient, compassionate, and self-aware individuals. By including the whole family, you create an environment where everyone thrives together. It's not just about parents teaching kids how to be mindful; it's about everyone—adults and children alike—coming together to support one another in this journey. This communal approach helps model mindfulness in a way that is both natural and impactful.

Start by integrating mindfulness into daily routines. These are moments shared by the family and can be the perfect opportunities to practice mindfulness together. For instance, you can begin with something as simple as a morning breathing exercise. Gather everyone in a quiet room, sit comfortably, and take five deep breaths together. This not only sets a positive tone for the day but also establishes a routine that everyone can look forward to.

A key aspect of building a family practice is maintaining consistency without rigidity. Flexibility is crucial because life with kids can be unpredictable. If the planned morning session doesn't happen, find another opportunity later in the day. Perhaps a quick mindfulness break before dinner or a short meditation session before bedtime. The goal is to make mindfulness a natural part of the family rhythm, not an added burden.

Storytime can be another wonderful avenue for mindfulness. Choose books that emphasize themes like being present, kindness, and understanding emotions. Reading these stories together, you can discuss the mindful lessons and relate them to real-life scenarios. This not only reinforces mindfulness concepts but also makes them relatable for children, enhancing their understanding and application.

Another important practice is mindful eating. Regular family meals are a great opportunity to slow down and savor the food together. Turn off the TV, put away the devices, and focus on each bite. Discuss the flavors, textures, and even the origins of the food. This simple practice not only turns meals into a sensory experience but also fosters gratitude and awareness.

Consider establishing a 'mindfulness corner' in your home. It could be a cozy nook with soft cushions, a few books, and maybe some calming scents like lavender. Encourage everyone to visit this corner when they need a moment of peace or simply want to practice their mindfulness exercises. This dedicated space can serve as a gentle reminder of the importance of taking care of one's mental well-being.

Physical activities like yoga can also be a shared mindful practice. Yoga for kids is fun and engaging, and doing it together as a family can enhance bonds and create joyful experiences. Try setting aside a day each week for a family yoga session. Start with simple poses and focus on breathing together. It's a wonderful way to connect on both physical and emotional levels.

When conflicts arise, use these moments as teaching opportunities for mindfulness. Encourage everyone to take a few deep breaths before reacting. This pause can help diffuse tension and bring clarity. Discussing emotions openly and mindfully as a family helps everyone understand each other better and promotes a culture of empathy and patience at home.

Building a family mindfulness practice also involves fostering an environment of non-judgment. Mistakes will happen, and that's okay. If someone forgets to practice or finds it difficult, approach the situation with compassion rather than criticism. This encourages a growth mindset that is essential for mindfulness to take root and flourish.

Incorporate mindfulness into family outings as well. Whether it's a walk in the park or a weekend hike, use these opportunities to practice being present. Ask the children to notice the colors of the leaves, the sounds of the birds, or the texture of the tree bark. These activities not only deepen their appreciation for nature but also teach them to find mindfulness in everyday moments.

It's equally important to involve children in the planning of family mindfulness activities. When kids feel they have a say, they're more likely to be engaged and enthusiastic. Let them choose a mindfulness story to read, a yoga pose to try, or even suggest a new activity. Their involvement fosters a sense of ownership and makes the practice more enjoyable for everyone.

Lastly, celebrate the small wins. Acknowledge the efforts everyone is putting into practicing mindfulness. Whether it's a child's first successful deep breath or a family member's thoughtful response in a stressful situation, these moments are worth celebrating. Positive reinforcement builds motivation and helps sustain the practice.

Creating a family culture of mindfulness is a rewarding journey that benefits everyone involved. It nurtures emotional intelligence, strengthens familial bonds, and fosters a supportive environment where each member can grow. Through shared experiences, consistent practice, and mutual support, you'll find that mindfulness becomes not just a practice but a way of life for your family.

Chapter 15: Mindfulness at Work

Imagine walking into a workplace where the clamor of tasks and endless meetings no longer feel like an uphill battle, but rather, an opportunity for growth and calm. Incorporating mindfulness at work isn't just about reducing stress—though that's a welcome side effect—it's about enhancing productivity and creating a more positive workplace environment. By taking a few moments throughout the day to focus on your breath or briefly meditate, you can reset your mental state, allowing you to approach tasks with newfound clarity and creativity. It's about fostering a culture where being present becomes the norm, energizing your focus and enlarging your capacity to handle challenges with grace. In essence, mindfulness at work is about turning the mundane into the meaningful, creating a ripple effect of well-being that touches every aspect of your professional life.

Reducing Workplace Stress

Workplace stress can feel like an inescapable part of modern life. Deadlines, meetings, and the constant ping of notifications can wreak havoc on your peace of mind. However, incorporating mindfulness at work offers simple yet powerful ways to alleviate this stress. It's not just about surviving the workday; it's about thriving within it.

First, let's talk about recognizing stress in the workplace. It's easy to overlook the signs due to the sheer busyness of the day. Often, we ignore what our bodies and minds are telling us. You might find yourself feeling irritable, exhausted, or overly anxious. Physical symptoms could include headaches, muscle tension, or digestive issues. Identifying these signs early can be the first step towards alleviating stress.

Imagine starting your day with a few minutes of mindful breathing before even turning on your computer. It's a simple practice: sit comfortably, close your eyes if you're not feeling self-conscious, and focus on your breath. Inhale deeply, hold it for a few seconds, then exhale slowly. This simple action can help center you, making you more resilient to the stresses of the day ahead.

Taking mindful breaks is another key strategy. Rather than scrolling through social media or answering emails during your break, take a few minutes just for yourself. Step outside if you can, or find a quiet room. Observe your surroundings, feel the air on your skin, or just focus on your breath. These micro-moments of mindfulness can refresh your mind and reduce stress.

Another technique is mindful listening. Meetings are often a hotbed for stress, especially if you're worried about contributing or managing the discussion. By practicing mindful listening, you shift your focus from your internal anxieties to fully engaging with the speaker. Listen without preparing your response while they're still talking. This not only reduces your stress but also makes you a more effective communicator.

Let's consider the physical workspace. Cluttered desks and chaotic environments are breeding grounds for stress. Take a moment to organize your space. Aim for simplicity and a sense of order. You don't have to go full minimalist, but reducing clutter can help clear your mind, making it easier to focus on your tasks.

Mindful time management is another tool. Multitasking might seem efficient, but it often leads to mistakes and stress. Instead, try to focus on one task at a time. Prioritize your tasks and tackle them in chunks. The Pomodoro Technique, where you work for 25 minutes and then take a 5-minute break, can be particularly effective. It blends productivity with mindfulness by acknowledging our brain's need for short breaks.

Let's not overlook the importance of mindful eating at work. It's tempting to scarf down lunch at your desk while you soldier on with your tasks. However, taking time to eat mindfully can serve as a powerful break. Savor each bite, notice the flavors, and chew slowly. This practice not only helps in digestion but also offers a pleasant pause in your workday.

Then there's the concept of gratitude. Workplace stress often comes from focusing too much on the negatives—missed deadlines, conflicts, or just the sheer volume of work. Taking a moment each day to jot down or think about things you're grateful for can shift your mindset. It doesn't have to be big things; even appreciating a cup of coffee or a supportive colleague can make a difference.

Also, mindfulness can be integrated into email management. Instead of replying to emails as soon as they come in, set specific times during the day to check and respond to them. This minor adjustment can free up mental space for deeper, more focused work.

The practice of mindful stretching can also be a savior. Sitting at a desk for long periods can lead to physical discomfort and stress. Taking a few moments to stretch can alleviate tension. Simple neck rolls, shoulder shrugs, and wrist stretches can make a significant difference in how you feel by the end of the day.

When things get particularly rough, mindful visualizations can provide an escape. Close your eyes and visualize a place where you feel completely at peace. It could be a beach, a forest, or a quiet room in your house. Spend a few minutes there in your mind. This mental escape can alleviate stress and bring a sense of calm.

Mindful collaboration can further enhance a stress-free environment. When working in teams, being mindful about communication, respecting boundaries, and fostering a culture of openness can mitigate a lot of stress. When everyone is on the same page, the workday can become less about racing against time and more about achieving collective goals.

Lastly, consider holistic work-life balance. Mindfulness doesn't end when you leave the office. Carrying these practices into your home life can create a seamless transition where stress doesn't get to invade your personal space. Engage in activities that nurture your soul—be it reading, gardening, or spending time with loved ones. The more balanced your overall life is, the less impact work stress will have.

In conclusion, reducing workplace stress through mindfulness isn't about overhauling your life overnight. It's about integrating small, manageable practices into your daily routine. Over time, these moments of mindfulness can accumulate, creating a more peaceful and focused work life. Embrace the journey and remember that even the smallest step towards mindfulness can lead to significant improvements in your well-being.

Enhancing Productivity

Imagine starting your day with a mind as clear as a still pond, an internal calm that allows you to tackle tasks with laser-like focus. This isn't a distant dream; it's a reality you can achieve through the practice of mindfulness. Think of how much more you'd accomplish if you let go of distractions, stress, and mental clutter.

Mindfulness cultivates an awareness that sharpens your focus, tone down distractions, and boosts your efficiency. When you're fully engaged in the present moment, those nagging thoughts about upcoming deadlines or uncompleted tasks fade away. You're simply here, now, working on the task at hand. This can make all the difference in the world when it comes to productivity.

Research has shown that our brains perform best when we single-task, and mindfulness teaches us to do just that. By regularly practicing mindfulness, you train your brain to stay focused on one task at a time. It breaks the cycle of multitasking—the bane of productivity—and centers your attention where it counts. Consistency in this practice will effectively lessen the habitual urge to juggle multiple tasks at once.

Implementing mindfulness in your daily routine can be as simple as starting your day with a few minutes of meditation. A brief session where you focus on your breath or engage in body scan meditation can set a tranquil tone for the day. You're not merely wading through a to-do list; you become deliberate and centered in your actions, allowing you to achieve more with less strain.

Let's delve into some practical techniques. A common and effective way to blend mindfulness with your workday is through the Pomodoro Technique.

This involves working for a set period, say 25 minutes, followed by a short break. During these breaks, a quick mindfulness exercise, like deep breathing or a short walk, can refresh and reset your focus. The simple act of stepping away and redirecting your awareness inward can significantly boost your cognitive performance and productivity.

Another helpful method is mindful email management. Set aside specific times during the day to check and respond to emails, and when you do, fully immerse yourself in the task. Read each email thoroughly, respond thoughtfully, and then move on. This reduces the constant 'ping' of email notifications that can pull your attention away from more important tasks.

Mindfulness also involves acknowledging and managing emotions that may hinder productivity. Becoming aware of feelings like frustration or impatience as they arise can prevent them from escalating. Instead of letting these emotions derail your work, you can address them through mindful breathing or a brief pause. This not only maintains your emotional balance but also ensures that your productivity remains steady.

If you're engaged in creative work, mindfulness can be exceptionally beneficial. The openness and focus cultivated in mindfulness practice can lead to more innovative solutions and ideas. When your mind isn't bogged down by stress or distracted by unrelated thoughts, it has greater capacity to think creatively.

Creating a mindful workspace is another step towards enhanced productivity. This involves organizing your environment in a way that minimizes distractions and supports your focus. A clutter-free desk, calming plants, and even a dedicated space for quick mindfulness exercises can make a noticeable difference in how productive you feel.

Consider incorporating mindfulness into meetings as well. Starting meetings with a few moments of silent focus sets a concentrated tone and encourages everyone to be fully present. This can lead to more efficient and effective discussions, decreasing the time spent in unproductive back-and-forths.

Mindfulness also promotes better time management. By being present, you're able to more accurately assess how long tasks take and plan more realistic schedules. You become more adept at prioritizing tasks, making it easier to focus on what's truly important rather than getting lost in a sea of minor obligations.

For those willing to explore deeper, integrating mindfulness apps can offer guided sessions that easily fit into busy schedules. Apps like Headspace or Calm provide short, targeted exercises designed to improve focus and mental clarity, perfect for a quick midday recharge.

One of the beautiful aspects of mindfulness is its flexibility. You don't have to adhere to a strict regimen to see benefits. Whether it's a brief meditation before diving into an important project, or a mindful break during lunch, these moments of focused awareness accumulate to create a significant impact on your productivity.

Tailoring these techniques to fit your personal workflow and preferences can enhance their effectiveness. Experiment with different practices and find what resonates most with you. The key is consistency; even small, regular practices can gradually shift your mindset towards a more focused and productive state.

Incorporating mindfulness into your work isn't just about getting more done; it's about working smarter and creating a harmonious balance between your professional and personal life. When you're mindful, you're not just ticking off tasks, you're engaging with them fully, leading to a deeper sense of accomplishment and satisfaction.

As you start to weave mindfulness into your day, you'll begin to notice how it complements your flow of work. With this growth in awareness, you'll find yourself naturally gravitating towards a more organized and efficient way of operating. Enhanced productivity will no longer be about the sheer volume of work completed, but about the meaningful engagement with each task.

So, take a mindful step forward. Begin with a simple practice, and let the awareness grow. Your productivity will thank you, and so will your sense of mental well-being.

Chapter 16: Meditation and Creativity

Unlocking your creative potential often seems like an elusive quest, but meditation can be the key to that treasure chest. By fostering a state of mindful awareness, meditation allows you to quiet the mental chatter, and in that stillness, creativity can flourish. Imagine clearing away the cobwebs, making way for fresh, innovative ideas to emerge. When you're faced with creative blocks, mindfulness helps you approach problems from different angles, seeing possibilities where before there were none. As you sit in stillness, ideas can float effortlessly to the surface, like leaves drifting on a pond. It's not about forcing creativity but rather creating the right environment for it to thrive. Meditation brings a sense of openness and curiosity, encouraging you to explore uncharted territories of your imagination. So, let's embrace the practice of meditation to cultivate a life rich with creativity and endless potential.

Unlocking Creative Potential

There's a profound connection between meditation and creativity. When we meditate, we are not only training our minds to focus and find tranquility; we are also creating the space for creative thoughts to emerge naturally. When the mind is cluttered with worries, to-do lists, and constant distractions, it struggles to think freely or creatively. By practicing meditation, we can clear away the noise, allowing our intrinsic creativity to flourish.

You might wonder how a simple act like sitting quietly can unlock creative potential. The answer lies in brain function. When we meditate, particularly through mindfulness practices, we engage the prefrontal cortex and reduce activity in the brain's default mode network (DMN). The DMN is associated with self-referential thoughts—essentially, the mind-wandering and chatter that frequently distract us. As this chatter quiets, there's more room for creativity and innovation to surface.

Consider this: the most innovative ideas often come to us when we're not actively trying to solve a problem. Think of the 'eureka' moments in the shower, during a leisurely walk, or just before falling asleep. Meditation cultivates a similar mental state, where the pressure to think is lifted, and our natural creativity can emerge.

Practices like open-monitoring meditation can be invaluable in fostering creativity. This form of meditation involves observing thoughts and emotions as they arise and pass, without attachment. By doing so, we disarm the mental blocks and anxieties that hinder creative thought. Creativity thrives in open and non-judgmental mental spaces, which mindfulness meditation can readily provide.

It's also important to recognize that creativity isn't confined to the realms of art, music, or writing. Creativity is the bedrock of problem-solving, innovative thinking, and even interpersonal relationships. Regardless of where your creativity lies, meditation can serve as a powerful tool to enhance it.

Let's discuss practical ways to tap into this potential. One effective method involves incorporating regular breaks in your daily routine strictly for mindful meditation. Activities like mindful breathing or body scan meditations can create mental clearings, offering a fresher perspective upon return to creative tasks. These brief, contemplative moments can act like mental resets, reviving your creative energies.

Another valuable practice is setting an intention before starting a meditation session. This intention could be a simple, open-ended question related to a creative project you're working on. For example, "What new perspective can I bring to my writing?" or "What unique solution can I find for this problem?" Hold this question lightly in your mind. As you proceed with your meditation, don't actively try to answer it. Allow your subconscious to work in the background, often leading to unexpected and innovative ideas later on.

Meditation also helps dissolve the fear of failure—a common barrier in creative endeavors. By nurturing a mindset that focuses on the present moment and accepts thoughts without judgment, you learn to embrace the process of creation instead of the outcome. This acceptance encourages experimentation and risk-taking, both of which are fertile grounds for creativity.

Additionally, group meditations can provide a different kind of creative stimulation. Engaging in a meditative practice with others can foster a sense of collective energy and inspiration. Whether it's through a guided session or a shared silent meditation, the communal experience can spark new ideas and perspectives, broadening your creative horizons.

The environment in which you meditate can also influence your creative capacity. Creating a mindful space with minimal distractions can help cultivate an atmosphere conducive to heightened creativity. This might include incorporating elements that inspire you—perhaps a piece of artwork, a plant, or soft lighting. The goal is to create a sanctuary that brings you peace and opens your mind to creative thoughts.

Beyond these practical steps, it's crucial to understand that cultivating creativity through meditation is an ongoing journey. Consistency is key. Just as creativity is a process, so too is meditation. Regular practice reinforces the mental pathways that allow creative thoughts to flourish. Over time, you'll find that moments of insight and inspiration become more frequent and accessible.

Remember, creativity is not a finite resource to be depleted. Rather, it is an ever-renewing wellspring that can be tapped into with mindful practice. Each meditation session, each moment of mindfulness, nourishes this wellspring. The more you engage with your practice, the more bountiful your creative potential becomes.

Ultimately, the synergy between meditation and creativity lies in their shared foundation of openness and presence. Meditation teaches us to observe without judgment, allowing us to see the world with fresh eyes. This perspective is the very heart of creativity, leading us to new ideas, solutions, and expressions. By cultivating a mindful practice, you are not just unlocking your creative potential; you are opening the door to a richer, more imaginative, and fulfilling life.

Using Mindfulness to Break Blocks

Creativity, that elusive gem, isn't always easy to come by. We've all faced moments when the ideas just don't flow, when the well of inspiration seems to have dried up completely. It's in these moments of stagnation that mindfulness can prove to be a powerful ally, helping us to break through the barriers that hold us back. Let's dive into how you can harness mindfulness to overcome creative blocks and unlock your full creative potential.

At its core, mindfulness is about being present. It's about tuning into your thoughts, feelings, and environment without judgment. When we hit a creative block, our minds often become a tangled web of worry, doubt, and frustration. These emotions can cloud our thinking and stifle our creativity. Mindfulness helps us to recognize these feelings and observe them without getting entangled in them. By stepping back and viewing things from a more detached perspective, we can begin to see our creative blockages more clearly and start dismantling them piece by piece.

Think about the last time you faced a creative block. You probably found yourself overthinking every little detail, second-guessing every idea. This hypercritical mindset can create a mental bottleneck. Mindfulness allows us to break free from this cycle by bringing our focus back to the present moment. Instead of getting lost in the maze of "what-ifs" and "should-haves," we learn to concentrate on the task at hand. This shift in focus can be incredibly liberating, allowing ideas to flow more freely.

One practical way to use mindfulness to break creative blocks is through a technique known as mindful breathing. When you find yourself stuck, take a few moments to close your eyes and focus on your breath. Feel the sensation of the air entering and leaving your nostrils. Notice the rise and fall of your chest. Breathe deeply and slowly, allowing yourself to become fully immersed in the experience. This simple practice can help to clear your mind, reduce stress, and create a mental space where new ideas can emerge.

Another effective technique is the body scan meditation. This involves bringing your attention to different parts of your body, one at a time, and noticing any sensations or tension. By shifting your focus away from your mental block and onto your physical self, you can release built-up stress and anxiety. This physical relaxation often translates into mental relaxation, making it easier for creativity to flow.

Journaling can also be a powerful tool when used mindfully. Set aside a dedicated time each day to write freely, without censoring yourself. Focus on the act of writing itself rather than the content. Don't worry about spelling, grammar, or coherence. The goal is to let your thoughts pour out onto the page without restraint. This process can help to bypass the critical part of your brain that often stifles creativity, allowing you to tap into your subconscious mind where your most original ideas reside.

It's also important to acknowledge and accept your creative block rather than fighting it. Often, our natural response to a blockage is to push harder, to force ideas to come. But this only increases tension and frustration. Instead, try simply acknowledging that you're experiencing a block. Accept it as part of the creative process. By doing so, you remove the power that the block holds over you. Mindfulness teaches us that it's okay to have periods of uninspired thought. These moments are just as much a part of the creative journey as the moments of high inspiration.

Mindful walking is another technique that can help to break creative blocks. When you feel stuck, take a walk outside. Pay close attention to the sights, sounds, and smells around you. Notice how your body feels with each step. This change of environment and intentional focus on the present moment can often lead to new insights and ideas. Movement has a way of shaking up our mental patterns and opening up new pathways for creativity to flow.

Group meditation sessions can also be beneficial. Being in a mindful space with others who are also focusing on their own inner worlds can create a collective energy that enhances individual efforts. Sharing this mindful silence with others can help dissolve your creative blocks by fostering a sense of shared purpose and connection. Sometimes, just knowing you are not alone in your struggle can be profoundly freeing.

Additionally, certain mindfulness practices encourage us to engage with our work in new ways. For instance, mindful drawing or doodling can be a surprisingly effective method for overcoming creative blockages. The act of drawing without a specific goal or purpose can free your mind from the pressures of "getting it right." This playful approach can often lead to unexpected bursts of inspiration and insight that might not surface through more conventional methods.

Let's not forget the power of a mindful mindset shift. Approach your creative work with a beginner's mind, a concept from Zen Buddhism that encourages seeing things as if for the first time. This fresh perspective can dismantle preconceived notions and habitual thought patterns that contribute to the blockages in your creative flow. You start to see possibilities and connections that were previously hidden because you were looking through the lens of past experiences and expectations.

Mindfulness is not about eradicating blocks altogether. Such an aim might be unrealistic. Instead, it's about learning to navigate these blocks more skillfully. When we become more mindful, we build resilience and develop a more compassionate relationship with ourselves. This self-compassion is crucial in moments of creative stagnation, providing the emotional cushioning needed to persist and eventually thrive.

Moreover, mindfulness isn't a one-time fix but rather an ongoing practice. The benefits accumulates over time, gradually rewiring your brain to be more open, less judgmental, and more at ease with the natural ebb and flow of creativity. Consistency is key. Set aside a few minutes every day to practice mindfulness, whether it's through meditation, mindful breathing, or any other technique that resonates with you. Over time, you'll likely find that these practices not only help you break through creative blocks but also enhance your overall sense of well-being.

Remember, every creative journey has its hurdles. Embracing mindfulness can make those hurdles less daunting and the path much clearer. When you integrate mindfulness into your creative process, you're not just finding ways to overcome blocks; you're enriching the entirety of your creative practice, making it more fulfilling and deeply satisfying. So, the next time you find yourself staring at a blank page or a stalled project, take a mindful breath, and know that the flow will return. With mindfulness, you have the tool to guide it back.

Chapter 17: Mindfulness During Difficult Times

In the midst of life's upheavals, practicing mindfulness can be a powerful anchor, grounding us when everything feels uncertain. Rather than getting swept away by the storm of emotions, mindfulness urges us to observe them with compassion and curiosity. It's not about erasing the difficulties but about facing them with a kind and steady presence. By tuning into the breath and the present moment, we can create a space within ourselves that fosters resilience and a greater capacity to cope with adversity. This mindful approach helps us navigate crises with a clearer mind and an open heart, reminding us that even in the hardest times, we hold the power to find our inner calm.

Coping with Crisis

Challenges and crises are inevitable parts of life. From personal setbacks to global events, our ability to cope using mindfulness can make a significant difference in how we navigate these turbulent waters. When faced with a crisis, it's easy to feel overwhelmed and helpless. However, mindfulness has tools to ground and guide us through even the most challenging times.

In moments of crisis, our minds often gravitate towards what-ifs and worst-case scenarios. These thought spirals can heighten our stress and anxiety, making it difficult to see the situation clearly. One of the first steps in coping with crisis through mindfulness is to bring our attention back to the present moment. By focusing on the here and now, we start to break the cycle of anxious thoughts and gain a clearer, more realistic perspective.

Mindful breathing is a powerful technique for coping with crisis. When emotions are running high, taking deep, deliberate breaths can anchor us. This not only helps calm the nervous system but also provides a much-needed pause before reacting. Practicing this simple technique can help us respond to crisis situations more thoughtfully and less impulsively.

Another essential aspect of coping with a crisis is self-compassion. It's common to be hard on ourselves when things go wrong, but negative self-talk can exacerbate stress. Mindfulness encourages us to treat ourselves with the same kindness we would offer a friend. By acknowledging our struggles without judgment, we create a supportive space that fosters resilience.

The crisis can also challenge our sense of control. Mindfulness teaches us to accept what we cannot change and focus our energy on what we can influence. This doesn't mean giving up or resigning ourselves to fate but rather adopting a practical and proactive mindset. Acceptance helps us conserve mental and emotional resources, allowing us to tackle problems more effectively.

Mindful observation is another valuable tool. During a crisis, paying close attention to our thoughts, emotions, and bodily sensations can provide insights into our internal state. This self-awareness can inform better decision-making and help us identify unhelpful patterns that may need addressing. For instance, noticing that our shoulders are tense can prompt us to relax and release some of that physical and emotional burden.

Sometimes, the way we cope during a crisis is by reaching out to others. While mindfulness emphasizes self-awareness, it doesn't exclude the importance of community and relationships. Sharing our experiences with trusted friends or family members can offer relief and perspective. Being mindful of our vulnerability and openness can deepen our connections and provide the support we need.

For some, a crisis can evoke a sense of loss or grief. Mindfulness allows space for these difficult emotions, encouraging us to sit with them rather than pushing them away. Through mindful acknowledgment, we validate our feelings, which can be a crucial step toward healing. It's about feeling all the layers of our emotions, which ultimately can lead to greater acceptance and understanding.

Certainly, not every crisis allows for calm reflection immediately. There are times when swift action is required. However, even in the midst of rapid responses, weaving in moments of mindfulness can help keep us centered. It might be as quick as taking a deep breath before making a crucial phone call or pausing for a moment to ground ourselves before entering a difficult conversation.

Mindfulness is also beneficial in the aftermath of a crisis. Once the immediacy has passed, taking time to reflect mindfully on what happened and how we responded can be invaluable. This reflection can teach us a lot about our strengths, areas for growth, and the effectiveness of our coping strategies. By learning from these experiences, we build resilience for future challenges.

Building and maintaining mindfulness practices during calm periods can also fortify us against the storms. Regular meditation, even in short sessions, strengthens our ability to stay present and manage stress. When a crisis does hit, those established mindfulness habits become crucial resources we can lean on.

Incorporating gratitude practices during crises might seem counterintuitive but can be profoundly uplifting. Acknowledging small moments of goodness—like the support of a friend or a moment of peace—can provide rays of light in dark times. Gratitude helps reframe our experiences, shifting focus from what's wrong to what remains right, offering a balanced perspective.

Finally, mindfulness cultivates a sense of impermanence and resilience. Crises, like all things, pass. By deeply understanding and internalizing this, we begin to see crises not as permanent setbacks but as temporary challenges. This perspective empowers us to move through difficulties with grace and a hopeful outlook.

Remember, mindfulness isn't about eliminating challenges but transforming our relationship with them. By integrating mindfulness into our lives, we create a toolbox of strategies to navigate crises more effectively and emerge stronger on the other side.

Building Resilience

In times of hardship, resilience can often feel like a distant, elusive quality that belongs to someone else. Yet, building resilience is not only possible for everyone, but it's also firmly rooted in the practice of mindfulness. Life throws curveballs, and sometimes it feels like you're perpetually in the ninth inning, facing the toughest pitcher imaginable. That's precisely when resilience matters the most.

Resilience isn't just about bouncing back; it's also about how we adapt, learn, and even thrive despite adversity. Mindfulness trains us to maintain emotional balance and focus. This doesn't happen overnight, but with consistent practice, it can be transformative. Consider mindfulness as the mental gym where resilience is your ultimate fitness goal.

Let's start with the basics—focusing on the present moment. Mindfulness encourages you to take life one step at a time, which can be incredibly grounding in moments of stress. This practice serves to remind us that we don't have to solve everything at once. It's about making measurable progress and, frequently, that's all we need to keep going.

One of the key facets of resilience is the ability to manage stress effectively. When faced with a crisis, our instincts often urge us to react quickly and decisively. While there are times when immediate action is necessary, knee-jerk reactions typically lead to more stress down the line. By practicing mindfulness, you cultivate the ability to pause and assess situations calmly, which can prevent emotional escalation and poor decision-making.

What does this look like in practice? It might be as simple as taking three deep breaths before responding to a triggering email. It's moments like these that build resilience over time. By slowing down, you give yourself the space to choose a mindful response rather than an automatic reaction.

An essential element of resilience is self-awareness. Mindfulness practices teach us to recognize our emotional states without judgment. When you can identify feelings of anger, sadness, or frustration as they arise, you're better equipped to manage them constructively. Self-awareness is like having a personal barometer for your internal weather, helping you navigate emotional storms more effectively.

Resilience also relies heavily on the mind-body connection. Studies show that physical health and mental well-being are closely linked. Mindfulness practices such as body scan meditation or mindful walking can help you stay in tune with your physical state. Being aware of how stress manifests in your body is the first step in addressing it.

Another aspect of building resilience is cultivating a growth mindset. Resilient individuals often view challenges as opportunities for growth rather than insurmountable obstacles. This perspective shift can be greatly enhanced by mindfulness. When you approach challenges mindfully, you're less likely to be paralyzed by fear or anxiety. Instead, you can focus on what can be learned from the experience.

Imagine facing a project with a tight deadline. Pressure mounts, and the initial reaction might be to panic. Through mindful practice, you can train yourself to break down the task into manageable steps. Each small victory builds confidence, reinforcing your resilience muscle. It's like turning a marathon into a series of sprints, reducing overwhelm and making the entire process more attainable.

An often overlooked yet vital component of resilience is fostering positive relationships. Mindfulness enhances our ability to connect with others on a deeper level, promoting empathy and effective communication. These strong social connections can serve as a support net during tough times, reminding us that we don't have to face challenges alone.

It's also important to acknowledge moments of personal achievement, no matter how small. Celebrating progress, even in the face of adversity, nurtures resilience by reinforcing the belief that you are capable. Mindfulness teaches us to appreciate the present and recognize these small victories, which can sustain us during challenging times.

Building resilience through mindfulness is also about fostering a sense of acceptance. Acceptance isn't about surrendering to adversity; it's about acknowledging the reality of a situation without letting it consume you.

When we accept our circumstances, we're better positioned to move forward constructively. This doesn't imply resignation but rather an understanding that adaptation is part of the journey.

Lastly, remember that building resilience is a continuous process. There will be setbacks, and that's okay. Mindfulness helps us understand that imperfection is a natural part of life's ebb and flow. Each setback is an opportunity to practice self-compassion and resilience. It's about showing up again and again, no matter how many times you fall.

Resilience doesn't shield us from life's difficulties, but it does provide us with the tools to navigate them with greater ease and grace. By integrating mindfulness practices into our daily lives, we build a robust framework that supports emotional and mental well-being. As we cultivate these habits, our capacity for resilience grows, empowering us to face any challenge head-on.

Adopting mindfulness practices to foster resilience can profoundly enhance your quality of life. The next time you find yourself in the midst of difficulty, remember that resilience is not a distant goal but a lifelong practice, nurtured one mindful moment at a time.

Chapter 18: Technology and Meditation

In today's fast-paced digital age, technology and meditation may seem like unlikely companions, but they can actually complement each other beautifully. Mindfulness apps have become invaluable tools for anyone looking to cultivate a regular meditation practice. With guided sessions, reminders, and progress tracking, these apps provide structure and support that can make meditation more accessible and consistent. However, it's also crucial to strike a balance and be mindful of our tech usage to avoid digital burnout. Embracing digital detox tips, like setting boundaries for screen time and incorporating device-free moments into your day, can help you reconnect with the present moment and reclaim your peace of mind. Leveraging technology wisely while maintaining mindful habits can enhance your journey towards reduced stress and improved focus.

Mindfulness Apps

In this digital age, where our smartphones often serve as an extension of ourselves, mindfulness apps have emerged as powerful tools to bring a sense of calm and focus into our daily lives. These apps offer guided meditations, reminders, and various techniques to help you stay present, all at your fingertips. While some might argue that true mindfulness doesn't require technology, there's a growing body of evidence that suggests these apps can be effective in reducing stress, improving mental clarity, and helping users achieve a greater sense of peace.

One of the most appealing aspects of mindfulness apps is their accessibility.

Whether you're a novice or a seasoned meditator, these apps provide a broad spectrum of practices that cater to different levels and preferences. You can find everything from quick, five-minute meditations to soothe anxiety, to more extensive programs designed to deepen your practice over several weeks. The convenience of having these resources available whenever you need them can't be overstated.

Take, for instance, apps like Headspace and Calm. These platforms have become nearly synonymous with digital mindfulness. Headspace was co-founded by a former Buddhist monk and offers a user-friendly interface that makes it easy to integrate mindfulness into your daily routine. Calm, on the other hand, provides a variety of features such as ambient sounds, sleep stories, and specific meditation courses that focus on everything from stress relief to enhancing focus. Both of these apps have free and subscription-based content, ensuring that there's something for everyone.

Breaking down some of the features of these apps can help us appreciate their value even more. Guided meditations, often led by experienced instructors, are one of the standout features. These sessions can vary in length and focus, offering users a chance to explore different meditation techniques without the need for in-person classes. For those who find it difficult to sit in silence, guided meditations can be an excellent way to stay engaged and focused.

Another invaluable feature of mindfulness apps is the ability to track progress. Most apps come with a journal or log to keep tabs on your sessions, noting how you felt before and after meditating. This can be particularly useful for identifying patterns or triggers in your emotional well-being. Over time, these insights can help you adjust your practice to better meet your needs and goals.

Beyond the guided meditations and progress tracking, many mindfulness apps also include breathing exercises. Learning to control your breath is fundamental to practicing mindfulness, and these exercises can range from simple, timed breathing to more advanced pranayama techniques. By incorporating these exercises into your routine, you can develop a greater sense of control over your physiological responses to stress.

Some might wonder if there's a downside to using technology to practice mindfulness. After all, aren't we trying to unplug and disconnect from our devices? It's a valid concern, but the key is balance. Using a mindfulness app doesn't mean you'll be glued to your phone. Instead, these tools can serve as helpful reminders to take a mindful moment, offering structure and guidance that are especially beneficial for beginners.

Moreover, many apps are designed with user experience in mind, minimizing distractions and maximizing engagement. Features like "Do Not Disturb" modes and customizable reminders can help you create a dedicated mindfulness practice that fits seamlessly into your life without causing additional screen time stress.

In addition, for those who prefer a more communal experience, several apps offer community features. These might include forums, discussion groups, or even live meditation sessions where you can practice alongside others. This sense of community can be incredibly motivating and provide a sense of shared journey, which is often missing in solitary practices.

The variety in content is another strong point. You can find specialized mindfulness sessions for different needs and situations — whether it's managing workplace stress, dealing with insomnia, or even handling difficult emotions. Some apps offer courses that focus on mindfulness for specific demographics like children, pregnant women, or athletes, ensuring there's a tailored approach for everyone.

Let's not overlook the abundance of free resources available. While many high-quality apps offer subscription services, there are plenty of free options that provide substantial value. For example, Insight Timer offers a vast library of free meditations and talks from mindfulness teachers around the world. This app also includes a timer feature for self-guided sessions and a social component where users can see how many others are meditating simultaneously.

Of course, with so many choices out there, it can be a bit overwhelming to decide which app is right for you. A good starting point is to consider what you want to achieve with your mindfulness practice. Are you looking for something that offers short, daily meditations? Or perhaps you're interested in more extensive programs that require a longer commitment? Reading reviews and testing out free trials can also help you get a sense of what each app has to offer and whether it resonates with you.

In conclusion, the integration of mindfulness apps into our daily lives provides an incredible opportunity to enhance mental well-being. These digital tools make mindfulness accessible to a wider audience, offering convenience, variety, and support that can enrich your meditation practice. Whether you're a beginner just starting out or looking to deepen your practice, there's likely a mindfulness app that can help guide you on your journey to greater peace and self-awareness.

Digital Detox Tips

In today's world, our lives are intertwined with technology. From the moment we wake up to the moment we go to sleep, screens demand our attention. Yet, as useful as technology can be for connectivity and productivity, it can also become a significant source of stress and distraction. Implementing digital detox strategies can help you harness the benefits of mindfulness and deepen your meditation practice.

Start by setting specific times throughout your day for a digital detox. Try beginning with an hour in the morning and an hour before bed. During these periods, put your phone on airplane mode, turn off notifications, and resist the urge to check your devices. These moments allow your mind to rest and reset, encouraging a naturally more mindful state.

Next, designate tech-free zones in your home. Your bedroom, for instance, should be a sanctuary for rest and relaxation, free of the digital noise that can disrupt your sleep and intrude on your mental peace. Consider creating a cozy meditation nook where technology isn't allowed, except maybe for a timer or calming music.

A practical tip for digital detoxing is to participate in activities that completely occupy your hands and mind, making it less likely for you to reach for your devices out of habit. Engage in gardening, cooking, or painting. These activities not only keep you busy but also naturally align with the principles of mindfulness, offering moments of focused attention and presence.

Cultivate the habit of single-tasking instead of multitasking. Multitasking with digital devices often leads to a fractured mind, reducing the quality of attention you can give to any one task. Single-tasking, on the other hand, allows you to immerse fully in the experience, whether it's eating a meal, having a conversation, or simply walking in nature. This practice strengthens your ability to maintain focus and enhances your meditation sessions.

Reflect on the content you consume digitally. Seek out content that enriches your life and supports your mental well-being. Limit exposure to negative news and social media that can induce stress or comparison. Instead, choose podcasts, articles, and videos that inspire growth, knowledge, and positivity. You'll find that mindful consumption of digital content aligns seamlessly with the goals of a digital detox.

Try incorporating 'Tech Sabbaths' into your week. Dedicate one day, typically a weekend day, to completely disconnect from technology. Use this day to immerse yourself in nature, spend quality time with loved ones, or engage in deep reflective practices. Tech Sabbaths create an extended window for mental rejuvenation, setting a balanced tone for the upcoming week.

Communication boundaries are essential. Let friends, family, and colleagues know ahead of time when you'll be offline. This clear communication helps manage their expectations and ensures that your digital detox practices don't lead to unnecessary stress or misunderstandings. It also serves as a subtle reminder to others about the importance of taking breaks from technology.

You might also find it helpful to assess which digital apps or services are enhancing your life and which are merely stealing your time. Conduct a digital audit, identifying and eliminating those apps that serve no meaningful purpose or contribute to stress. Replace them with tools that support mindfulness, like guided meditation apps or those that help you track your mood and habits.

Establish a mindful morning routine that doesn't involve checking your phone first thing. Instead, start your day with a short meditation, journaling, or simply sitting quietly with a cup of tea. This sets a calm and reflective tone for the day, allowing you to carry the tranquility of morning mindfulness throughout your daily activities.

Balancing screen time throughout the day can also aid in reducing overall digital fatigue. Schedule specific times for checking emails and social media, rather than allowing them to interrupt you constantly. This structured approach helps maintain focus and prevents the feeling of being perpetually 'on-call'.

Lastly, consider the impact of blue light exposure from screens, especially in the evening. Blue light can interfere with your sleep patterns, making it harder to achieve restful sleep. Use blue light filters on your devices or switch to reading a physical book before bed. This small change can significantly improve the quality of your sleep, thereby enhancing your overall well-being.

Remember, the goal of a digital detox is not to reject technology entirely but to establish a healthier, more balanced relationship with it. By creating these mindful habits, you're more likely to experience a deeper sense of peace and presence, both in your meditative practice and in your daily life.

Incorporating these digital detox tips isn't about perfection. It's about progress, making small, consistent changes that collectively lead to a more mindful and balanced way of living. Start where you are and with what feels most manageable. Over time, you'll find that these practices become second nature, significantly enhancing your mental well-being.

Your mind and body will thank you for the break, and your meditation practice will flourish as you cultivate spaces of stillness and presence amidst the digital noise. Embrace the journey of digital detoxing, and witness how it transforms not only your meditation but your overall perspective on life.

Chapter 19: Creating a Sustainable Practice

Building a sustainable mindfulness practice isn't just about the initial excitement or the first few sessions of meditation; it's about making mindfulness an integral part of your daily life. The key is to set realistic goals that align with your lifestyle, ensuring that your practice can flourish even on the busiest days. Start small, perhaps with just five minutes a day, and gradually increase as you feel more comfortable. Keep track of your progress, not as a means to judge yourself, but to celebrate your growth and stay motivated. Journaling can help you notice subtle shifts in your mental and emotional landscape, acting as a gentle reminder of why you started this journey in the first place. Most importantly, remember that mindfulness is not about perfection but about presence. Approach each session with kindness towards yourself, and let go of any expectations of what your practice "should" look like. This compassionate mindset will help you persist through challenges and create a lasting, meaningful practice.

Setting Realistic Goals

Setting realistic goals is crucial when it comes to creating a sustainable mindfulness practice. Without attainable objectives, it's easy to feel overwhelmed and disheartened, which can lead to giving up altogether. But with thoughtful planning and a little patience, you can set yourself up for long-term success.

First and foremost, identify what you want to achieve through your mindfulness practice. Are you looking to reduce stress, enhance focus, or cultivate a deeper sense of peace? It's important to have a clear intention because this will inform your goals and keep you motivated. Remember, the goal is not to become a monk overnight but to make consistent, incremental progress.

Once you've nailed down your overarching objective, break it into smaller, actionable steps. For example, if your goal is to meditate daily, start with just a few minutes each session instead of jumping straight into hour-long sittings. This is akin to training for a marathon; you wouldn't start by running 26 miles on day one. Gradually increasing your meditation time allows you to build the habit without feeling overwhelmed.

Another key element in setting realistic goals is to be specific. Vague commitments like "I want to meditate more" are less effective than "I will meditate for 10 minutes every morning." Specificity turns your intention into a concrete plan, making it easier to track progress and hold yourself accountable. Write your goals down in a journal or a planner to create a tangible reminder of your commitment.

Flexibility is also essential. Life happens, and some days you might not be able to stick to your plan. Maybe an unexpected meeting pops up or your morning routine gets disrupted. Instead of throwing in the towel, adjust your goals to fit your circumstances. If you miss your morning meditation, try to find ten minutes during lunch or before bed. Remember, the aim is consistency over perfection.

Incorporating milestones into your goal-setting process can be tremendously rewarding. Celebrating small victories gives you a sense of achievement and keeps you motivated. Perhaps you set a milestone to meditate for ten consecutive days or to practice mindful eating for a week. Reward yourself with something that feels special but doesn't counteract your mindfulness objectives, like a relaxing bath or a hike in nature.

Tracking your progress can be a game-changer. Maintaining a log of your practice sessions provides invaluable insights into your journey. You may want to jot down what you did, how long you meditated, and how you felt before and after. Over time, you'll notice patterns and trends that can help you fine-tune your goals and strategies.

Accountability is another tool that can significantly enhance your success.

Sharing your goals with a friend or joining a mindfulness group can provide that extra layer of commitment. When others know about your objectives, you're more likely to stick to them. It can also be encouraging to discuss your progress and challenges with like-minded individuals who understand what you're going through.

It's important to balance ambition with self-compassion. Be your own cheerleader, not your harshest critic. If you miss a day or find it challenging to focus, remember that it's all part of the process. Each moment is a new opportunity to begin again. Mindfulness is about being present, not perfect.

Consider the long-term benefits rather than short-term gains. Sustainable mindfulness practice is a lifelong journey, and short-term setbacks don't define your overall progress. Keeping the bigger picture in mind will help you stay committed even when you hit bumps along the road.

Another effective strategy is to integrate your mindfulness practice into your existing routines. If sitting down to meditate feels daunting, try mindful walking, eating, or even mindful showering. By incorporating mindfulness into activities you already do, you make it a natural part of your life rather than an additional task on your to-do list.

Meditation and mindfulness apps can also provide structured programs and reminders to keep you on track. Features like progress tracking, guided sessions, and community support can be invaluable as you work towards your goals. While technology shouldn't replace self-motivation, it can certainly complement your efforts.

Lastly, revisit and reassess your goals periodically. What worked initially might need tweaking as you grow in your practice. Be open to change and willing to adapt. Maybe you initially aimed to meditate every morning but find that evenings work better for you. Adjusting your goals based on your experiences and lifestyle changes ensures that they remain relevant and attainable.

The journey of creating a sustainable mindfulness practice is unique to each individual. Setting realistic goals tailored to your needs and circumstances is essential for long-term success. By breaking down your objectives, being specific, tracking progress, and remaining flexible, you'll build a strong foundation that supports lasting mindfulness in your life.

Tracking Progress

Creating a sustainable mindfulness practice isn't just about starting strong; it's equally about monitoring how far you've come and tweaking your approach along the way. After all, what gets measured gets managed. Tracking progress allows you to reflect on your journey, celebrate the small victories and identify areas for improvement. This section will offer practical advice on how to track your mindfulness practice in a way that's encouraging and enlightening.

First things first: let's talk about journaling. A mindfulness journal can be as simple or as elaborate as you want it to be. The key is consistency. Dedicate a few minutes daily to jot down your experiences, emotions, and observations. This exercise serves multiple purposes. It helps unload your thoughts, thereby clearing mental clutter, and gives you a tangible record of your progress.

Within your journal entries, try to note specific things like the length of your meditation sessions, techniques used, and how you felt before and after. Over time, you might notice patterns. For instance, perhaps mornings are better for you, or maybe guided meditations offer more clarity than silent sessions. These insights are invaluable for refining your practice. You don't have to write a novel; even a few bullet points will do the trick.

Another efficient way to track your mindfulness journey is through apps built specifically for this purpose. Many of these applications are designed to log your meditation sessions, track your mood over time, and even remind you to practice. They often include features that allow you to set goals and see your improvement graphically. Some popular options include Headspace, Calm, and Insight Timer.

Accountability can also play a significant role in ensuring you stay on track. Sharing your goals and progress with a mindfulness buddy or a meditation group creates a support system where encouragement and shared experiences can bolster your commitment. This isn't about competition but rather harnessing the power of community to lift each other up.

Visual aids like calendars and habit trackers can also be exceedingly beneficial. Creating a simple chart where you mark off each day you meditate can be surprisingly motivating. It gives you a quick snapshot of your commitment level and can be immensely satisfying as you see the streaks grow longer.

Interval check-ins are another fantastic tool for tracking progress. Schedule periodic reviews—once a week, bi-weekly, or monthly—where you sit down and evaluate your practice. Ask yourself questions like: "What changes have I noticed in my stress levels?", "Am I more focused throughout the day?", or "Have I become better at regulating my emotions?" Write down your reflections and aim to be as honest and objective as possible.

Keeping an eye on qualitative aspects is just as important as noting quantitative ones. While it's easy to count the minutes of meditation, also ask yourself how the quality of these sessions is evolving. Are you finding it easier to reach a state of calm? Are distractions less frequent? How about your awareness and presence during the sessions—has it deepened?

Goal-setting should not be ignored when discussing tracking progress. Set realistic yet challenging goals for your practice. These can be as simple as extending your meditation time gradually or as comprehensive as integrating mindfulness into various aspects of your daily life. Having these goals provides direction and purpose, and achieving them, no matter how small they might seem, can be incredibly encouraging.

Moreover, don't be afraid to experiment with different tracking methods until you find what works best for you. Some people thrive on detailed data and charts, while others might prefer a more minimalist approach. There's no one-size-fits-all here; the goal is to find a method that keeps you motivated and informed.

If you find yourself struggling or hitting a plateau, consider changing up your practice. Maybe try a different form of meditation, tweak your routine, or participate in a workshop. Reflecting on your progress can provide clues on what changes might be beneficial. For example, if you notice your enthusiasm waning, joining a local meditation group might rekindle your passion.

Remember, it's essential to be kind to yourself. Progress in mindfulness isn't always linear. Some days you might feel like you've taken three steps forward, and other days it might feel like two steps back. That's okay. The very act of showing up and practicing is progress in itself.

Lastly, don't forget to celebrate your achievements. Whether it's completing a month of daily meditations or noticing a significant reduction in stress, acknowledge your efforts and give yourself credit. Rewards don't have to be extravagant; even something simple like a cup of your favorite tea or extra leisure time can be a nice gesture to appreciate your hard work.

Incorporating these tracking techniques can enrich your mindfulness journey, offering both insight and inspiration. Tracking your progress bridges the gap between where you started and where you want to go, making your path toward mental well-being all the more clear and attainable.

When you document your journey and reflect on it, you build a deeper connection with your practice. This relationship is what sustains and nurtures your ongoing mindfulness efforts. Each entry, each mark, each reflection serves as a testament to your commitment to enhancing your mental well-being.

Chapter 20: Mindfulness in Nature

Spending time in nature offers a profound opportunity to practice mindfulness and reconnect with our inner selves. The rhythmic sounds of rustling leaves, the gentle breeze, and the symphony of bird songs are not just beautiful; they serve as natural anchors, pulling us into the present moment. As you walk through a forest or sit by a stream, let your senses guide you—feel the earth beneath your feet and smell the fresh, invigorating air. Nature provides a sanctuary away from the constant buzz of everyday life, allowing you to ground yourself and find tranquility in the simplicity of the natural world. Engaging in outdoor meditation or simply being mindful during a nature walk can significantly enhance your mental well-being, grounding you and offering a refreshing perspective on life's worries. Don't underestimate the power of the great outdoors; it's nature's own way of inviting us to breathe deeply, pause, and just be.

Outdoor Meditation Techniques

Embracing meditation outdoors provides a unique opportunity to connect more deeply with the natural world. Nature has an uncanny way of grounding us, fostering inner peace, and sharpening our focus—all elements crucial to an effective mindfulness practice. Picture yourself sitting under a sprawling tree or beside a gently flowing stream, the symphony of nature guiding your breath and thoughts. Let's dive into some effective meditation techniques you can practice outdoors.

One of the easiest ways to begin outdoor meditation is the "Nature Attunement" technique. Find a quiet spot, sit comfortably, and close your eyes. Start by focusing on your breath, inhaling slowly through your nose and exhaling through your mouth. Gradually shift your awareness to the sounds around you—birds chirping, leaves rustling, water trickling. Let these natural sounds anchor your meditation, helping you to remain present and centered.

For those who enjoy a bit of movement, "Walking Meditation" offers a perfect blend of mindfulness and physical activity. Choose a path that is serene and relatively free of distractions. Walk slowly and deliberately, focusing on the sensations of each step—the way your heel touches the ground, the roll of your foot, the push-off with your toes. Synchronize your breath with your steps, creating a rhythmic, meditative pace. This technique enhances your connection to your surroundings, deepens your breath, and calms your mind.

Seated or standing, another powerful method is "Sky Gazing." This technique involves simply looking up at the sky—whether it's a vast expanse of blue, a canvas of stars, or a dance of clouds. Allow the vastness of the sky to remind you of the expansive nature of your own mind. Breathe deeply, and with every exhale, imagine releasing a bit of tension, letting it dissipate into the sky. This practice not only relaxes you but also expands your perspective, helping you to see challenges as part of the larger picture.

Then there's the "Tree Connection" meditation, a grounding practice where you use a tree as a focal point. Find a tree that resonates with you. Sit or stand close to it, placing your hands gently on its bark if you wish. Close your eyes and visualize the tree's roots extending deep into the earth. Imagine your own body growing roots, intertwining with the tree's roots. With each breath, feel the strength and stability of the tree flow into you, grounding you and offering a sense of resilience.

Another charming practice is the "Flower Meditation." Find a flower that captures your interest. Sit comfortably at eye level with the flower and focus all your attention on it. Observe every detail—the color, the texture, the way it sways in the breeze. This technique sharpens your focus and brings a profound appreciation for the small beauties of life, often overlooked in our daily rush.

For water lovers, "Water Watching" can be an incredibly soothing practice. Whether it's a river, lake, or the ocean, water has a natural meditative quality. Sit or stand by the water and simply watch its movement. Pay attention to the patterns and the sounds. If you're near the ocean, you might align your breath with the rhythm of the waves. This connection to water can have a calming effect on your mind, washing away stress and tension.

"Sensory Meditation" is another valuable technique, especially potent in nature. Sit comfortably and close your eyes. Begin by focusing on your breath, then gradually open your awareness to each of your senses one by one. Start with the sounds around you, then move to the sensations on your skin—the warmth of the sun, a gentle breeze. Open your eyes and take in the colors and shapes around you. This technique helps to immerse you fully in the present moment, making you more attuned to the richness of your surroundings.

Let's not forget the synergistic effect of combining breathwork with nature. Techniques like "Nature Breathing" can amplify mindfulness. Find a nature spot that feels right, sit or stand comfortably, and breathe in sync with the environment. As you inhale, imagine drawing in the freshness and vitality of nature. As you exhale, visualize releasing stress and negative energy into the ground beneath you. This cyclical exchange can rejuvenate your energy and deepen your meditative state.

For those who crave a communal experience, group meditations in nature can be immensely fulfilling. Gather a group of like-minded individuals and choose a quiet, natural setting. Begin with simple breathwork or a guided meditation, allowing everyone to sync with nature and each other. The collective energy can be incredibly powerful, creating a shared sense of peace and mindfulness that is deeply rewarding.

Finally, consider the seasons and how they influence your meditative experience. Each season offers unique sights, sounds, and sensations that can enrich your practice. Spring's new growth, summer's vibrant life, autumn's falling leaves, and winter's stillness all provide diverse environments for meditation. Allow the characteristics of each season to inspire and guide your mindfulness.

Outdoor meditation is not just about practicing techniques; it's about forming a relationship with Mother Nature. It's about feeling the earth beneath your feet, hearing the whispers of the wind, and seeing the inter-connectedness of all living things. Whether you're looking to reduce stress, improve focus, or achieve a deeper sense of peace, integrating these outdoor meditation techniques into your routine can profoundly enhance your mental well-being.

Mindfulness in nature isn't just an escape from the hustle and bustle of daily life. It's a return to a natural state of being—where peace, clarity, and connectedness are readily accessible. So, the next time you seek tranquility or wish to deepen your practice, step outside. Let nature be your guide.

Nature Walks

There's no denying the profound sense of peace that washes over us when we're immersed in nature. Whether it's a stroll through a local park or a hike in the mountains, nature walks offer a special kind of mindfulness practice that can deeply enhance our mental well-being. By connecting with the earth beneath our feet and the sky above, we're given the opportunity to anchor ourselves in the present moment in a visceral, tangible way.

Engaging in nature walks isn't just about getting from point A to point B. Instead, it's about opening ourselves up to the rich tapestry of sensations, sights, and sounds that the natural world presents. As we walk, we can focus on the rhythmic crunch of leaves underfoot, the interplay of sunlight and shadows through the trees, and the subtle movements of wildlife. Each step becomes a conscious act of mindfulness, grounding us in the here and now.

A nature walk brings an element of adventure and discovery to mindfulness. Every path, whether familiar or new, can reveal surprises—perhaps a curious squirrel, a blooming flower, or an unexpected vista. These moments of beauty and wonder aren't interruptions; they're integral to the mindfulness practice, inviting us to appreciate the intricacies of life around us. They remind us that we are part of something larger, something profoundly interconnected.

One technique to deepen mindfulness during a nature walk is to engage all of our senses. Start by pausing occasionally to take a few deep breaths, letting the crisp, clean air fill your lungs. Notice the scents—maybe the sweet aroma of wildflowers or the earthy smell after a rain shower. Listen closely: the rustling leaves, birds singing, or even a distant stream gurgling. Feel the textures around you—perhaps the roughness of tree bark or the coolness of a stone. Observing these details helps to center our minds and anchor our awareness.

It's also beneficial to walk slowly and deliberately, almost as if moving in slow motion. This pace allows our minds to slow down in sync with our bodies. When we walk mindfully, we notice the subtleties of our movements—how our feet make contact with the ground, how our weight shifts from one leg to the other. It transforms what could be a routine physical activity into a rich, meditative experience.

Another approach is to integrate brief moments of stillness into your walk. Find a spot that speaks to you and take a moment to stand or sit quietly. This simple act of being still in nature can be incredibly calming. It's a chance to let go of any mental chatter and tune into the natural rhythm of the environment. Watch a cloud drift across the sky or observe the gentle swaying of branches in the breeze. Stillness in nature can serve as a potent reminder of the beauty of simply being.

Group nature walks can also be a powerful way to cultivate mindfulness. Walking in silence with others can create a shared sense of presence and connection. It's a collective journey where spoken words are replaced by mutual awareness and appreciation for the natural world. This shared experience can deepen our sense of community and belonging, enhancing our mental well-being in the process.

For those who have access to varied landscapes, changing up the scenery can keep nature walks fresh and engaging. Rivers, forests, meadows, and mountains each offer their own unique experiences and challenges. By exploring different environments, we cultivate adaptability and openness, key components of a mindful mindset. Moreover, each new setting provides novel stimuli for our senses, making it easier to stay engaged and present.

It's essential to recognize that nature walks offer a space for self-reflection. Away from the bustle of daily life, the quietude of nature can help clarify our thoughts and emotions. This reflective space allows us to process experiences, make peace with our challenges, and celebrate our achievements. It's a time to check in with ourselves, to nurture our inner world alongside the outer one.

Eventually, the practice of mindfulness during nature walks can extend beyond the walk itself. The skills we develop—being present, observing without judgment, and appreciating the moment—begin to permeate other areas of our lives. We find ourselves carrying the calm and clarity we cultivated on our walks into our homes, workplaces, and relationships. This holistic integration of mindfulness helps to foster a sustained sense of peace and equanimity.

Incorporating nature walks into our routine doesn't require monumental shifts. It's about consistently carving out time, even if it's just a few minutes, to step outside and engage with the natural world. Over time, these small, regular practices can build up, contributing significantly to our overall mental health. And importantly, nature walks are accessible to most of us, making them a practical and effective tool for enhancing well-being.

In conclusion, nature walks represent a harmonious blend of physical activity and meditative practice. They invite us to slow down, breathe, and immerse ourselves in the beauty and tranquility of the natural world. By mindfully engaging with nature, we can unlock new levels of relaxation, insight, and connection. Whether we're traversing rugged trails or wandering through a city park, each walk holds the potential to enrich our minds and nourish our souls.

Chapter 21: Spiritual Aspects of Mindfulness

Mindfulness, at its core, can be a deeply spiritual practice that transcends religious boundaries and connects us to something greater than ourselves. Whether you associate spirituality with a higher power, inner wisdom, or simply a profound sense of interconnectedness, integrating mindfulness into your spiritual life can cultivate a richer, more meaningful existence. It's about embracing the present moment with openness and curiosity, allowing us to explore our personal beliefs and experiences more deeply. This union of mindfulness and spirituality often leads to profound insights and a sense of peace, giving us the strength and clarity to navigate life's challenges with grace. As you advance in your mindfulness journey, consider how these practices can intertwine, enhancing both your spiritual awareness and your overall well-being.

Exploring Personal Beliefs

As we dive into the spiritual aspects of mindfulness, it's important to acknowledge that personal beliefs often shape our experience and understanding of meditation. Everyone embarks on this journey with their own set of beliefs, whether they're rooted in religion, spiritual practices, or philosophical ideas. The beauty of mindfulness is its adaptability; it can be molded to fit within the framework of your pre-existing beliefs or help you cultivate new ones.

Our personal beliefs act as the lens through which we view the world. These beliefs can significantly influence the way we approach mindfulness. For instance, someone with a Christian background may incorporate prayer as a form of mindfulness, seeking a sense of divine presence in their practice. On the other hand, a person with a more secular viewpoint might approach mindfulness purely as a mental health tool without any spiritual overtones.

Consider for a moment how your beliefs have shaped other areas of your life. Have they provided comfort during tough times? Have they offered a sense of purpose or direction? Bringing the same reflective inquiry to your mindfulness practice can help illuminate the intersections between your personal beliefs and your mindfulness journey.

Now, it's okay if your beliefs challenge or even conflict with the teachings of mindfulness at first. This dissonance can actually be a fertile ground for growth. It encourages introspection and invites you to explore why you hold onto certain beliefs and how they serve you. In some cases, you might find areas where your beliefs and mindfulness practices can enrich each other, creating a more holistic approach to well-being.

Imagine sitting in meditation and noticing a recurring thought or feeling related to your beliefs. Instead of brushing it aside, allow yourself to explore it with curiosity. Ask yourself questions like, "Why does this thought keep coming up?" or "What can I learn from this feeling?" This opens up a dialogue between your mind and spirit, often leading to profound insights and personal growth.

It's also worth noting that mindfulness itself can become a belief system. For many, the principles of mindfulness—such as non-judgment, acceptance, and compassion—transform into guiding tenets that influence daily life choices. While mindfulness doesn't require you to abandon your existing beliefs, it offers a complementary set of values that can harmonize with and even enhance those beliefs.

Integrating your personal beliefs with mindfulness isn't about adhering to strict rules. Instead, it's about finding harmony between the two. This might mean customizing your practice to reflect your spiritual values. For example, if walking in nature feels sacred to you, incorporating mindful walking in a natural setting can deepen both your spiritual and mindfulness practice.

Understanding that your personal beliefs will evolve over time is also key. As your mindfulness practice deepens, you may find that your beliefs shift or take on new meanings. This is a natural part of growth. Being open to this evolution can make your journey all the more enriching.

One practical way to explore this is through journaling. Reflecting on your meditation sessions and jotting down any insights related to your beliefs can offer clarity. You might write about a moment of deep connection you felt during a meditation, or a conflict between your mind's chatter and your spiritual teachings. Over time, this journal becomes a treasure trove of personal insights, marking your spiritual growth.

There will be times when doubt seeps in. You might question the validity of mindfulness or its ability to coexist with your beliefs. During such times, seeking guidance from a mentor or a community can be invaluable. Whether it's a religious leader, a spiritual guide, or a mindfulness teacher, having someone to discuss your journey with can offer new perspectives and reassurance.

Building a community around your practice can also be incredibly nourishing. Joining a meditation group that shares your beliefs or participating in a mindfulness workshop tailored to your spiritual framework can provide a sense of belonging and motivation.

To wrap this up, let's remember that the exploration of personal beliefs within mindfulness is a deeply personal journey. It's about allowing yourself the freedom to question, to seek, and to grow. There's no right or wrong way to integrate your beliefs with your practice—instead, it's about finding what works for you and walking that path with an open heart and mind. Embrace this journey, knowing that every step you take brings you closer to a more enriched and fulfilled sense of self.

Integrating Spiritual Practices

When exploring the spiritual aspects of mindfulness, integrating spiritual practices can serve as a profound way to deepen your connection with yourself and the present moment. Spiritual practices are not limited to any one particular faith or tradition. They can be customized to fit your belief system or personal preferences. By weaving spiritual practices into your mindfulness routine, you can enrich your experience and perhaps uncover new layers of meaning and understanding.

One way to start integrating spiritual practices is by incorporating prayer or chanting into your meditation sessions. If you follow a specific religious tradition, you might use prayers or chants from your tradition. For others, chanting can be as simple as repeating a meaningful phrase or word. This can help anchor your mind and elevate your practice from a simple mental exercise to a sacred ritual.

Journaling is another spiritual practice that can effortlessly blend with mindfulness. After a meditation session, take a few moments to jot down your thoughts, feelings, or any insights you gained. This reflective practice allows you to connect deeply with your inner self and can reveal patterns or areas that need attention. Keeping a journal can also serve as a historical record of your spiritual journey, offering you a way to look back and measure your growth over time.

Many traditions emphasize the importance of gratitude, which can be a powerful addition to your mindfulness practice. Creating a daily gratitude routine, where you consciously acknowledge the things you are thankful for, can shift your focus from what is lacking to what is abundant in your life. This simple yet potent practice aligns your energy with positivity and opens your heart to greater joy and contentment.

Another way to weave spiritual practices into your mindfulness is by engaging with nature. Many spiritual traditions regard nature as a divine creation that offers endless opportunities for reflection and connection. Simple activities like a mindful walk in the park, sitting by a river, or even tending to a garden can serve as acts of meditation. These experiences can help you feel grounded and more connected to the world around you.

Silence and solitude are often overlooked but are powerful spiritual practices in their own right. Carving out time for silent contemplation can help you connect more deeply with your inner wisdom. Whether it's a few minutes each day or a longer retreat, moments of silence can lead to profound insights and a deeper sense of peace. This practice can also enhance your ability to listen—to yourself, to others, and to the world around you.

You can also explore the concept of service as a form of spiritual practice. Acts of kindness and compassion not only benefit others but also enrich your own soul. Volunteering, helping a neighbor, or even small gestures like a smile or a kind word can be profound spiritual acts that bring your mindfulness practice into the real world.

Traditional ceremonies and rituals can offer a structured way to integrate spirituality with mindfulness. These can range from lighting a candle and setting an intention before meditation to participating in communal religious services. Rituals create a sense of sacredness and can provide a framework that helps you stay committed to your spiritual journey.

Breathwork, or pranayama, is another practice that can bridge the gap between spirituality and mindfulness. Focusing on your breath can anchor you in the present moment, and when done with intention, it can also open up channels of spiritual energy. There are various breathwork techniques you can explore, each with its own benefits, from calming the mind to energizing the body.

Mantras are powerful spiritual tools that can be easily incorporated into mindfulness practice. A mantra is a word or phrase that you repeat to yourself, either silently or out loud, to help focus your mind and connect with a deeper state of awareness. The mantra can be anything that resonates with you, whether it is a traditional phrase from a spiritual tradition, or something more personal and meaningful to you.

For those who enjoy artistic expression, creating art can be another form of spiritual practice that complements mindfulness. Drawing, painting, or even crafting can become meditative acts when approached with mindfulness. Focus on the process rather than the outcome, and let your creativity flow without judgment. This practice can be incredibly healing and can help you express things that words cannot capture.

Ultimately, integrating spiritual practices into mindfulness is a deeply personal journey. There is no right or wrong way to do it; what matters most is that it resonates with you and enriches your experience. Start with one practice, see how it feels, and gradually incorporate others. Remember, the goal is to deepen your sense of connection—with yourself, with others, and with the world around you.

By incorporating these spiritual practices, you'll likely find that your mindfulness journey becomes more fulfilling and impactful. The aim is not to overload yourself with new rituals, but to find simple yet powerful ways to bring a sense of sacredness into your everyday life. These practices are tools that can help you connect more deeply with your inner self, offering a richer, more nourishing meditation experience that transcends the ordinary and touches the divine.

Chapter 22: Stories of Transformation

I n this chapter, we delve into the awe-inspiring journeys of individuals who have harnessed mindfulness to transform their lives. Imagine Sarah, who once felt overwhelmed by her career demands but now finds solace in daily meditation practices, which have not only improved her focus but also brought a sense of peace. Or consider Tom, who struggled with chronic stress until he adopted mindful breathing exercises, significantly reducing his anxiety and making room for joy in his life. These personal stories, paired with insights from experts, serve as powerful reminders that mindfulness isn't just a practice; it's a journey of self-discovery and resilience. You'll find that these transformations, marked by struggles and breakthroughs alike, hold valuable lessons and inspirations for anyone seeking to enhance their mental well-being.

Personal Journeys

Transformation doesn't happen overnight. It's a gradual process where mindful practices slowly, but surely, shape one's life. One of the most compelling aspects of mindfulness and meditation is the profound impact it can have on an individual's journey. These personal stories of transformation can often provide a beacon of hope and inspiration to those just beginning their own practice.

Take Jessica, for instance. Jessica was a high-powered executive, always on the go, perpetually stressed out, and struggling to balance her career with her family life. She initially approached mindfulness with skepticism, dismissing it as "hippie nonsense." However, the mounting pressures of her job left her with no choice but to search for relief. She started with just five minutes of mindfulness meditation each morning, focusing on her breath and attempting to clear her cluttered mind. Within weeks, Jessica noticed a shift. She was less reactive, more patient, and found herself enjoying her time with her children rather than thinking about her next work meeting. Her colleagues noticed the change too, commenting on her newfound calmness in high-stress situations. For Jessica, mindfulness was not just a practice, but a path to reclaiming her life.

Then there's Mark, a college student juggling multiple responsibilities. Between attending classes, holding down a part-time job, and maintaining a social life, Mark felt like he was swimming upstream every day. The stress became overwhelming, affecting his grades and personal relationships. A friend introduced him to mindfulness meditation as a way to cope. Initially, Mark struggled to sit still and still his mind, but he persisted. Over time, the practice helped him develop a routine that brought clarity and focus to his day. Mindfulness taught him the importance of being present, and as his practice deepened, he found that he could concentrate better during study sessions and approach exams with a calm, collected mind. Just as importantly, his relationships improved as he became more empathetic and attentive to the people around him.

Let's not forget about Ella, a recently retired teacher who felt a sudden void in her life without the daily structure and purpose that her career provided. She turned to mindfulness as a way to navigate this new chapter. Ella started attending local meditation workshops and reading books on the topic. She found solace in the simplicity of mindfulness practices like mindful walking and deep breathing. Over time, Ella discovered a deep sense of peace and contentment within herself. Her journey also led her to volunteer at a local community center, where she now teaches mindfulness techniques to others, helping them deal with their own life transitions.

Rahul's story is another powerful example. As a tech entrepreneur, Rahul's life revolved around tight deadlines, constant innovation, and the pressure to outperform competitors. The tech industry's fast pace left him drained and mentally exhausted. A chance conversation with a colleague introduced him to the concept of mindfulness and its potential benefits for mental clarity and stress reduction. Rahul decided to give it a try, starting with basic breath awareness exercises during his breaks at work. Gradually, he integrated mindfulness into his daily routine, using it to stay grounded amidst the chaos of his professional life. The results were significant—he gained a newfound ability to make thoughtful decisions under pressure, fostered a more creative mindset, and ultimately saw an improvement in his company's performance.

From a different angle, there's Jasmine, a single mother working multiple jobs to support her family. Jasmine constantly felt overwhelmed, anxious, and disconnected. Her introduction to mindfulness was through a free community program aimed at helping individuals manage stress. Despite her initial doubts, Jasmine attended the sessions and committed to the practice with hope and determination. Over time, mindfulness became her anchor. She learned to find pockets of calm in her hectic days and managed her anxiety more effectively. Jasmine's children noticed the difference, too, benefiting from the positive atmosphere at home. The practice didn't solve all her problems, but it gave her the tools to approach life's challenges with a clear mind and an open heart.

Maya, a healthcare professional, faced burnout after years of working long shifts in a high-stress environment. She felt emotionally drained and disconnected from her purpose. A fellow nurse introduced her to mindfulness as a potential remedy. Skeptical yet desperate, Maya began incorporating short mindfulness exercises into her daily routine. She found that even a few minutes of focused breathing or a moment of silent reflection during her breaks made a significant difference in her stress levels. The practice also allowed her to reconnect with her initial passion for helping others, bringing a renewed sense of empathy and purpose to her work.

The transformative power of mindfulness is not limited to any specific background or set of circumstances. Whether you're a business mogul, a student, a retiree, or someone facing significant life challenges, mindfulness has the potential to effect profound changes. These personal journeys underscore a universal truth: that mindfulness and meditation, though simple in concept, hold the potential to unlock deep and lasting transformation. Their stories are testaments to the practice's ability to foster inner peace and resilience, no matter what life throws at you.

These personal accounts showcase the diverse ways in which mindfulness and meditation can play a pivotal role in one's journey towards mental well-being. They highlight that the path is personal and unique for each individual, yet the destination—greater peace, focus, and self-awareness—is a shared goal. While the journey may seem daunting at first, these stories illustrate that with commitment and openness, anyone can achieve meaningful transformation. The shared experiences remind us that we're not alone in our struggles and that there is a powerful tool available to help navigate them.

As you reflect on these stories, consider where you are in your own journey. What are the challenges you're facing, and how might integrating mindfulness into your daily routine help? Even the smallest step can set the wheels of transformation in motion. Remember, it's not about achieving perfection but about making progress. The journey of mindfulness is ongoing and ever-evolving.

The incredible variety and depth of these personal journeys stand as a testament to the versatility and accessibility of mindfulness practice. No matter where you are starting from, mindfulness offers a powerful pathway to enhanced mental well-being. Let these stories inspire and motivate you to begin or deepen your own practice, knowing that transformative change is possible.

Ultimately, the common thread running through all these stories is the profound impact mindfulness has on one's quality of life. Whether it's finding peace amidst chaos, improving relationships, or reclaiming a sense of purpose, the benefits are far-reaching. Each journey is a unique testament to the power of being present, living mindfully, and embracing each moment to the fullest.

Expert Testimonies

Expert testimony brings a unique depth to our understanding of mindfulness — it isn't just a personal anecdote or a fleeting trend, but a practice grounded in research and affirmed by leaders in various fields. These experts, coming from diverse professional backgrounds, share how mindfulness has transformed their lives and the lives of those they've worked with. So, let's dive into the profound insights and experiences of some of these thought leaders.

Dr. Susan Locke, a leading psychologist, recalls a poignant moment early in her career when she encountered a patient suffering from severe anxiety. Traditional therapies hadn't been effective. Desperate for a solution, she introduced mindfulness-based interventions. The impact was almost immediate. Her patient's anxiety lessened, their ability to handle stress improved, and their overall outlook on life became noticeably more positive. Dr. Locke mentions, "I saw firsthand how mindfulness wasn't just calming but a crucial tool for psychological resilience." Her practice soon integrated mindfulness as a core component, benefiting countless others.

Similarly, John Erickson, a veteran corporate executive, faced extreme burnout from a high-pressure job. Deadlines loomed constantly, and the ever-present demand to outperform competitors took its toll. Stressed and on the brink, he turned to mindfulness upon a colleague's suggestion. Erickson's introduction to mindful practices marked a turning point not only in his professional life but also in his personal well-being. He discovered that mindfulness allowed him to remain focused, make clearer decisions, and, surprisingly, improve the productivity of his entire team. "Mindfulness helped me realize that pausing isn't a waste of time. It's an investment in our mental bandwidth and clarity," Erickson emphasizes.

Academic circles, too, have widely recognized the benefits of mindfulness. Dr. Emily Johnson, an educator at a prominent university, saw significant improvements in students who practiced mindfulness. Faced with academic stress and personal challenges, these students often struggled to keep up. Dr. Johnson introduced brief mindfulness exercises at the start of her classes. The results were astonishing — better concentration, reduced stress levels, and enhanced academic performance. She noted, "Mindfulness doesn't only aid the individual practicing it but fosters a more attentive and compassionate classroom environment."

The realm of sports has also seen a burgeoning interest in mindfulness. Coach Rick Martinez, whose football team had faced consistent defeats, began collaborating with a mindfulness trainer. Initially skeptical, Martinez noticed profound changes as the season progressed. Players demonstrated better focus, teamwork, and a remarkable decrease in game-day anxiety. Martinez reflected, "It wasn't just about physical preparedness. Mindfulness provided a mental edge, the kind of mental strength that turned tight games in our favor."

Additionally, health professionals have weighed in on the transformative power of mindfulness. Nurse Cynthia Wallace recounts her experience with patients post-surgery. Managing pain and anxiety post-operation is crucial. Wallace began incorporating simple mindfulness techniques, such as guided breathing and body scans, into her patients' care plans. The results were immediate improvements in pain management and overall recovery. "Patients who engaged in mindfulness healed faster and showed more optimistic attitudes towards their recovery. It was a compelling validation of mindfulness in medical care," Wallace explains.

On the front lines of innovation, tech industry leaders are also advocates of mindfulness. Steve Green, a software developer, found his work becoming increasingly stressful. Constantly tethered to devices and deadlines, his mental wellness was suffering. Green turned to mindfulness apps, which led him down a path of deeper practice. Over time, he noticed not only a reduction in his stress levels but also a surge in creativity and problem-solving skills. "The clarity that mindfulness brings is unparalleled. It's like clearing the fog from your mind. My coding and problem-solving abilities were enhanced because I was present and focused," Green shares.

In the world of art and creativity, mindfulness has played a crucial role as well. Painter and sculptor Ava Collins attributes her surge in creativity and the emotional depth of her work to mindfulness. When faced with creative blocks, Collins practices mindfulness to center herself, allowing ideas to flow freely.

She states, "Mindfulness allows me to connect deeply with my emotions and thoughts, turning them into colors and forms that resonate with others. It's an artist's best-kept secret."

For those tackling life's most challenging adversities, mindfulness has proven to be a lifeline. Dr. Kevin Brown, an oncologist, has integrated mindfulness into his practice with terminally ill patients. Dr. Brown found that mindfulness helps patients find peace, manage pain, and cope with their emotions as they navigate their diagnosis. "Mindfulness provides them with a tool to live fully, even in their final days, offering serenity in the storm of their illness," Dr. Brown notes.

Notably, mindfulness has found its place even among those working in justice. Police officer Maria Hernandez, stationed in a high-stress urban environment, turned to mindfulness to manage the intense pressure of her job. Through mindfulness, she found a way to maintain her composure during high-tension situations, improving her decision-making and interactions with the community. Hernandez reflects, "Mindfulness has given me the mental clarity and calm needed to serve my community better and ensure my well-being."

Educational reformists like Principal Dan Michaels have also embraced mindfulness, incorporating it into school programs. These initiatives have led to decreased behavioral issues and enhanced student engagement. "The difference is tangible. Our students are not just well-behaved but genuinely happier and more attentive. Mindfulness is the foundation of a positive school culture," Michaels asserts.

These expert testimonies across various fields — from medicine, education, and corporate life to sports, technology, and art — illustrate the tremendous and far-reaching impact of mindfulness. Each story underscores the versatility and power of mindful practices, which aren't confined to meditation cushions but extend into every facet of life. Mindfulness isn't just a tool; it's a profound shift in living, offering unparalleled benefits for our mental well-being.

The takeaway from these testimonies is clear: mindfulness is a transformative practice that brings enduring benefits. Whether you're an executive, athlete, artist, educator, or healthcare professional, the practice of being present and mindful has the potential to uplift and invigorate your life. It's a testament to the idea that regardless of our roles and challenges, mindfulness can help us navigate the complexities of modern life with grace and clarity.

Chapter 23: Mindfulness and Physical Fitness

I ntegrating mindfulness into your physical fitness routine can transform the way you experience movement and exercise. It's not just about breaking a sweat or reaching a new personal best—it's about being fully present and engaged with your body. Whether you're lifting weights, running, or practicing yoga, mindfulness can elevate your workout by enhancing your focus, reducing stress, and fostering a deeper connection with yourself. Mindful exercise encourages you to listen to your body's signals, respect its limits, and celebrate its strengths, all the while cultivating a sense of inner peace and clarity. By staying in the moment, you make each movement intentional and impactful, creating a harmonious blend of mental and physical well-being that extends beyond the gym and into your everyday life.

Combining Exercise and Meditation

Combining exercise and meditation might seem like blending oil and water at first, but the union can be transformational for your mind and body. Imagine reaching a state of mental clarity while your body thrives in its physical peak. That's the beauty of integrating mindfulness into your fitness routine.

One simple way to merge these practices is through mindful breathing during exercise. Whether you're running, lifting weights, or practicing Pilates, focusing on each breath not only enhances your physical performance but also keeps your mind grounded. It's an opportunity to tune in to your body's signals—acknowledge the strain, feel the strength, and appreciate the movement.

Take running, for instance. Instead of zoning out or getting lost in thought, you can focus on the rhythm of your breathing in sync with your strides. Feel the ground beneath your feet, the wind against your skin, and the beating of your heart. This turns a routine jog into a meditative experience, allowing for deeper mental engagement alongside the physical activity. It's about transforming the mundane into the extraordinary by fostering a heightened sense of presence.

Similarly, during strength training, the concept of mindfulness can be incredibly impactful. As you engage in each lift or squat, focus on the muscles in action, the tension, and your form. This awareness can prevent injury and ensure you're getting the most out of each movement. When you lift with intention, it's not just about physical strength but mental resilience as well.

Yoga, traditionally a melding of mindfulness and physical exercise, exemplifies this synergy perfectly. Through its practice, you're not just stretching and strengthening your muscles but also cultivating a sense of inner peace and balance. Yoga encourages you to synchronize breath with movement, blending meditation seamlessly into physical exertion. Each pose becomes not just a physical challenge but a mediation in itself, allowing for reflection and mindfulness.

High-intensity interval training (HIIT) might seem like an unlikely candidate for mindfulness. But even in the chaos of high energy and rapid movements, there is room for awareness. During the short bursts of intense exercise, focus on the power and agility of your body. In recovery periods, bring your attention to calming your breath and heart rate. This ebb and flow create a dynamic field for meditation, honing both mental and physical acuity.

For some, group classes may serve as a perfect environment to explore this blend. Whether it's spinning, dance, or boot camp, the integration of mindfulness practices can enhance the communal and motivational aspects of the workout. Pay attention to the camaraderie, the collective energy, and the shared goal, all while staying present within your own experience.

Outdoor activities provide another beautiful setting for combining exercise and meditation. Imagine hiking through a forest trail. Each step becomes a deliberate action, each inhalation filled with fresh air, and each exhalation a release of tension. The natural surroundings offer a sensory-rich environment that amplifies the meditative quality of the exercise. The sound of leaves crunching underfoot and the sight of towering trees can serve as anchors for your mindfulness practice.

Mindful cycling is another noteworthy example. As you pedal, pay attention to your body's symmetrical motion, your legs' propulsion, and the rhythm of your heartbeat. The road before you becomes a visual meditation, and every curve, incline, and descent an exercise in focus and balance. This integration not only boosts your physical endurance but fortifies your mental stamina.

But what if you prefer the confines of a gym or home? Mindfulness can be practiced in such controlled environments too. On a treadmill, for instance, notice the mechanics of your stride and the steady rhythm it creates. Allow your breath to guide you, and keep your thoughts grounded in the present moment. Even in a small space, the scope for mental expansion is limitless.

Combine meditation with stretching routines post-exercise. As you cool down, let each stretch be a moment of deep mindfulness. Focus on the release of tension in each muscle group, observe your breath, and feel the interplay between effort and relaxation. This not only aids physical recovery but extends the benefits of meditation beyond a static seated practice.

Incorporating mindfulness into exercise is also a way to tackle common mental barriers. Often, we struggle with motivation, fatigue, or stress before a workout. By embedding meditative practices into your routine, you create a holistic approach that acknowledges and works through these barriers. For instance, start your session with a brief centering exercise—a moment of stillness to set your intention. This primes your mind and body for the activities ahead, making the exercise feel less like a chore and more like a conscious choice.

Let's not forget the enormous benefits this holistic approach brings. Merging exercise with meditation can significantly reduce stress, improve focus, and enhance overall well-being. Physical activity releases endorphins, the body's natural stress relievers, while meditation promotes relaxation and mental clarity. Together, they create a powerful synergy which nurtures both physical health and mental peace.

Another profound aspect is the development of self-awareness through this combination. Exercise, when done mindfully, brings immediate attention to your body's limitations and strengths. Meditation complements this by fostering acceptance and non-judgment. This balanced perspective is pivotal in achieving a healthier relationship with your body and mind.

Even more interesting is the influence this practice can have on your life off the mat or out of the gym. The discipline and awareness cultivated through mindful exercise seep into other areas of life, promoting better habits, enhancing productivity, and improving emotional regulation. It becomes a foundation upon which a more mindful, and fulfilling, life can be built.

So, how do you start this transformative journey of combining exercise and meditation? Begin with small steps. Introduce moments of mindfulness into your current routine. Gradually extend those moments as you become more comfortable. Don't worry about getting it perfect. The beauty lies in the practice itself—the continuous growth, the deeper insights, and the joy of movement and stillness blending harmoniously.

In summary, the integration of exercise and meditation offers a unique pathway to enhancing your mental and physical well-being. By weaving mindfulness into your physical routines, you're honing your body and enriching your mind. This combination is not just about fitness; it's a holistic approach to living a more balanced, aware, and enriched life.

Yoga and Mindfulness

Imagine a practice that weaves the body and mind into a harmonious tapestry of presence. That's yoga and mindfulness for you. This ancient practice has stood the test of time and remains relevant. When we talk about yoga in the context of mindfulness, we are looking deeper than the physical postures; we are diving into the unity of mind-body awareness.

Many people think of yoga as a purely physical practice, a series of challenging poses that sculpt the body. However, yoga, at its core, is a practice of mindfulness. The word "yoga" itself means union, referring to the connection between body, mind, and spirit. This connection is where the magic lies. By incorporating mindfulness into yoga, we can transform our approach to both.

Each pose, or asana, in yoga becomes an opportunity to observe and connect with our body's sensations, our breath, and our mental state. When holding a pose, notice the intricate play between effort and ease. Is there tension in your shoulders? Are you holding your breath? Mindfulness invites you to be curious, to explore these sensations without judgment.

Consider starting with a simple seated pose, such as Sukhasana, or "Easy Pose." Close your eyes, and bring your awareness to your breath. Inhale deeply and exhale fully. With each breath, allow yourself to settle more deeply into your body. This is mindfulness in action—being fully present in the experience, breath by breath.

Transitioning from one pose to another is also an opportunity to practice mindfulness. Instead of rushing through your yoga sequence, move slowly and deliberately. Pay attention to the way your muscles engage, the way your joints move, and the rhythm of your breath. This slow, mindful movement can turn even the simplest yoga practice into a powerful meditation.

Mindfulness in yoga isn't limited to the physical practice. It extends to your mental state as well. During your practice, thoughts will inevitably arise. That's perfectly okay. The goal is not to stop thinking but to notice when your mind has wandered and gently bring your attention back to the present moment. Over time, this practice can help you cultivate a sense of calm and clarity that extends beyond the yoga mat.

The combination of yoga and mindfulness can be particularly effective for stress reduction. Yoga helps to release physical tension, while mindfulness helps to calm the mind. Together, they provide a comprehensive approach to managing stress. Studies have shown that practicing yoga and mindfulness can lower cortisol levels, reduce anxiety, and improve overall well-being.

Another aspect to consider is the mindful integration of breath work, or pranayama, into your yoga practice. Focusing on your breath while performing yoga enhances your awareness and deepens your practice. Each inhale and exhale becomes a point of focus, grounding you in the present moment. This synergy between movement and breath brings a sense of balance and peace.

Yoga and mindfulness can also improve your focus and concentration. By regularly practicing mindful yoga, you train your brain to stay present and focused, which can enhance your ability to concentrate in other areas of your life. This is particularly beneficial for those of us who struggle with wandering thoughts or distractions.

Beyond the physical and mental benefits, yoga and mindfulness also offer a spiritual dimension. For many practitioners, the practice of yoga becomes a journey of self-discovery and spiritual growth. Mindfulness helps to cultivate an inner awareness that can guide you toward a deeper understanding of yourself and your place in the world.

If you're new to yoga and mindfulness, start small. You don't need to commit to a 90-minute practice every day. Even just a few minutes of mindful yoga can make a difference. Begin with a few simple poses, focusing on your breath and body sensations. As you become more comfortable, you can gradually extend your practice.

Incorporating yoga and mindfulness into your daily routine can be a game-changer. You might find that you move through your day with more ease and mindfulness. You become more aware of your body, your breath, and your mind. This awareness can spill over into other areas of your life, helping you to stay present and focused, even in the midst of stress and chaos.

Of course, like any practice, yoga and mindfulness require patience and consistency. You can't expect to see dramatic results overnight. But with time and dedication, you will likely find that these practices bring a sense of balance, peace, and resilience into your life.

For those already familiar with yoga, try deepening your practice by incorporating more mindful elements. Pay closer attention to your breath, your body, and your mental state. Explore different styles of yoga and see how they impact your mindfulness. Perhaps try a slower, more meditative style such as Yin Yoga or explore the flowing sequences of Vinyasa with a focus on mindful transitions.

Remember, yoga and mindfulness are practices, not destinations. There's no "right" way to do it. The beauty of these practices lies in their adaptability. Whether you're holding a challenging pose or simply sitting and breathing, you're engaging in mindfulness. And that, in itself, is a victory.

In conclusion, yoga and mindfulness offer a powerful combination for enhancing mental well-being. By bringing mindfulness into your yoga practice, you can deepen your connection to your body and mind, reduce stress, improve focus, and cultivate a greater sense of inner peace. It's a journey worth taking, one breath at a time.

Chapter 24: Global Perspectives on Mindfulness

I t's fascinating to see how mindfulness transcends cultures and borders, manifesting uniquely yet universally. From the serene tea ceremonies of Japan to the rhythmic breathing techniques of indigenous tribes in South America, each practice offers a window into the values and experiences of diverse communities. In India, mindfulness finds its roots in ancient yoga and meditation practices, imparting a sense of spirituality and oneness. Meanwhile, Scandinavian countries integrate mindfulness into daily life with a specific focus on simplicity and connecting with nature. As we explore these varied approaches, we discover a common thread: the pursuit of inner peace and the improvement of mental well-being. These international anecdotes not only enrich our understanding but also inspire us to adapt and personalize our mindfulness journeys. So, take a moment to reflect on how these global practices can complement and enhance your own path to mindfulness.

Cultural Practices

Mindfulness isn't a one-size-fits-all practice. Across the globe, various cultures have cultivated unique approaches to mindfulness that reflect their traditions, beliefs, and lifestyles. These cultural practices provide a rich tapestry of techniques and perspectives that can enhance our own understanding and experience of mindfulness.

Throughout Asia, mindfulness has deep historical roots, often entwined with spiritual and religious practices. In Japan, for instance, the tea ceremony, or "chanoyu," is much more than a social event; it is a spiritual ritual that embodies mindfulness. Participants focus intently on the precise movements, the aroma of the tea, and the serene environment. Every detail is noticed and appreciated, fostering a deep sense of presence and peace.

Similarly, in India, the concept of mindfulness, or "sati," is integral to many traditional practices like yoga and meditation. The ancient practice of yoga, widely popular today, originally aimed to prepare the mind and body for meditation. Breathing exercises ("pranayama") and bodily postures ("asanas") are practiced with mindfulness, ensuring that practitioners remain present and attentive to each movement and breath. This holistic approach intertwines body, mind, and spirit.

Moving to the Middle East, Sufi whirling, performed by the Mevlevi order of Sufis, is a form of active meditation. The whirling dervishes spin gracefully to the rhythm of spiritual music, focusing intently on their movement and breath. This dance aims to reach a state of mystical ecstasy and union with the divine. For the Sufis, it's a powerful way to cultivate mindfulness through a deeply spiritual and communal practice.

In the indigenous cultures of the Americas, mindfulness is often incorporated into everyday life through ceremonies and rituals. Native American smudging, for instance, involves burning sacred herbs like sage to purify the mind, body, and surroundings. The act of smudging is done with intention and awareness, invoking a prayerful state that cultivates mindfulness and connection to the Earth.

Heading over to Africa, traditional healing and mindfulness are intertwined in many cultural practices. For example, in South Africa, the practice of "Ubuntu," which emphasizes community, shared humanity, and compassion, plays a significant role in everyday life. Ubuntu encourages mindful living by fostering deep connections with others and promoting a sense of belonging and empathy.

In contrast, in the fast-paced modern cities of the West, mindfulness practices are often adapted to fit busy lifestyles. In European countries, you'll find people practicing mindfulness in more contemporary settings, such as during daily commutes, at work, or in structured group sessions. The popularity of mindful eating workshops and urban meditation centers speaks to the Western desire to slow down and find moments of peace amid the hustle and bustle.

Australia and New Zealand have also embraced mindfulness, particularly through the lens of nature. Indigenous Australian practices often emphasize a deep connection to the land, an awareness that is inherently mindful. "Dreamtime" stories and rituals encourage individuals to cultivate a strong, mindful relationship with nature, seeing it as a living, breathing entity that one is a part of.

Moreover, the mindfulness movement has found a comfortable spot in modern lifestyle projects around the globe. From Scandinavian "hygge," which encourages finding comfort and contentment in simple pleasures, to Italy's "Dolce far Niente," the sweetness of doing nothing, these cultural concepts inspire a mindful approach to daily life. They teach us that mindfulness doesn't always require formal meditation; sometimes, it's about finding joy in the present moment, whether that's through sipping tea, watching the sunset, or enjoying a quiet evening by the fire.

The beauty of these diverse cultural practices is that they reveal the universal desire for mindfulness, peace, and presence. Each practice, whether it's a formal meditation or a daily ritual, offers a unique window into how different cultures understand and cultivate mindfulness. This diversity reminds us that mindfulness isn't confined to a specific method or tradition; it's a flexible, adaptive practice that can be personalized to fit our individual lives and cultural contexts.

So, as you explore mindfulness, consider looking beyond your immediate surroundings. Experiment with practices from other cultures. Find what resonates with you and incorporate these techniques into your day-to-day. The essence of mindfulness is the same whether you're in a tea room in Japan, whirling with Sufis, or practicing yoga in India: it's about being fully present in the moment, honoring it with your complete attention and presence.

Ultimately, integrating these varied cultural practices into your own mindfulness journey can provide fresh perspectives and renewed inspiration.

You may discover that the simple act of being mindful carries a profound, universal power that connects us all, transcending borders and bridging different ways of life. So, allow yourself to be open to these rich traditions from around the world, and let them enhance your own practice in meaningful ways.

International Anecdotes

When we examine mindfulness across the globe, we unearth a treasure trove of stories; anecdotes that highlight how this practice is interwoven into the tapestry of various cultures. These narratives demonstrate mindfulness in unique, sometimes surprising, ways, reflecting the diversity of human experience. The beauty of this global perspective is that it reveals the universal language of mindfulness, transcending geographical and cultural boundaries.

In Japan, mindfulness takes shape in the form of tea ceremonies, or "chanoyu". This meticulous ritual isn't just about drinking tea; it's a philosophical and meditative practice. Each movement in the ceremony is performed with intentionality and presence. The host and guests focus on each step, from the precise way the tea powder is scooped to the measured pouring of water. This centuries-old practice is a powerful illustration of mindfulness—bringing one's full attention to the present moment. A participant once shared that even the simple act of wiping the tea bowl can bring profound peacefulness, as all thoughts narrow into that single, deliberate action.

Traveling to India, we encounter mindfulness through the ancient practice of yoga. Though yoga is often seen in the West as a mere form of physical exercise, its roots are deeply spiritual and meditative. In the quiet villages of Rishikesh, you'd find locals beginning their day with "Surya Namaskar" (Sun Salutation), blending breath, movement, and awareness into a harmonious routine. Practitioners describe feeling a sense of unity between their body, mind, and the universe, a holistic mindfulness that starts as the first light of dawn touches the Ganges River.

In the highlands of Peru, the indigenous Quechua people embody mindfulness in their relationship with nature. Living in harmony with their environment, every task they perform—from cultivating crops to weaving textiles—becomes an act of mindfulness. An elderly Quechua farmer once remarked that while he worked, he could feel the "heartbeat of the Earth," and this connection enabled him to stay grounded and present. This mindfulness isn't limited to moments of solitude; it's a communal experience woven into the fabric of their daily lives.

Meanwhile, the Maori of New Zealand integrate mindfulness through the concept of "whakapapa," which acknowledges one's genealogy and connection to all beings and things. Maori elder recounts spending dusk hours in contemplation, feeling profound mindfulness through this spiritual practice. Such acts help in fostering a deep respect for ancestry and self-awareness, highlighting how mindfulness interlaces with communal values and traditions.

Similarly, in African cultures, mindfulness finds its way through drumming and dance rituals. In Ghana, traditional "Adow" dances offer a vivid representation. Participants engage in rhythmic movements that synchronize with beats from handcrafted drums, creating a meditative state through collective energy. An elderly drummer mentioned how the beats echo the rhythm of the human heart, drawing everyone present into a focused, unified mindfulness.

Over in the Middle East, Sufism—a mystical branch of Islam—provides a rich soil for mindfulness practices. Whirling dervishes in Turkey are practitioners who seek to be closer to God through spinning in a meditative dance called "Sema." This whirling is not just a physical act but an immersive experience that connects the dervishes with their inner selves and the divine. It is said that during these moments, time itself seems to stand still, offering a glimpse into the boundless realms of mindfulness.

In Norway, a form of outdoor mindfulness known as "friluftsliv," which translates to "open-air living," encourages spending time in nature. Norwegians often hike, ski, or simply sit in the outdoors, immersing themselves fully in the present moment. One family shared that their weekly "friluftsliv" practice has become a sacred time for them to disconnect from digital distractions and reconnect with each other and nature. It underscores the idea that mindfulness doesn't always need a structured practice; sometimes, it's about savoring the simplicity of being in nature.

Diving into the Aboriginal cultures of Australia, we discover the tradition of "Dadirri," a form of deep, inner listening and reflection. For the Aboriginal people, Dadirri is a way to connect with their ancestral land and stories. Miriam-Rose, an Aboriginal elder, speaks about the significance of Dadirri as being akin to a meditation, a practice that promotes profound mindfulness. She describes it as listening not only with your ears but with your whole being, echoing a sense of unity and peace.

Across the ocean in Hawaii, "Ho'oponopono" portrays a different facet of mindfulness aimed at healing and reconciliation. This ancient Hawaiian practice involves gathering families to discuss and resolve conflicts. Guided by a kahuna, or priest, participants share their feelings openly and strive to restore harmony. The mindfulness here is in the act of listening and the sincere intention to heal relationships, providing emotional and spiritual cleansing.

As we make our way around the globe, it becomes clear that although the expressions of mindfulness vary, the core intent remains the same— to cultivate a deeper awareness and connection to life. These international anecdotes offer more than just insight into diverse practices; they serve as powerful reminders that mindfulness is an inclusive, adaptable practice available to anyone, anywhere.

Whether you're silently savoring a cup of tea in Japan or feeling the pulse of the Earth in Peru, these stories invite you to see mindfulness through a wider lens. Embrace the diversity, and let these global practices inspire your own journey toward mental well-being. Mindfulness, in all its forms, reminds us that despite our varied backgrounds, we share an innate desire for peace and presence.

Chapter 25: The Future of Mindfulness

The future of mindfulness is brimming with exciting possibilities that promise to revolutionize how we perceive and practice this age-old wisdom. We're seeing emerging research that delves deeper into the neuroscientific underpinnings of mindfulness, offering fresh insights into its profound effects on mental well-being. While traditional practices continue to hold timeless value, innovations such as virtual reality meditations and AI-driven mindfulness coaches are breaking new ground, making mindfulness more accessible and personalized than ever before. As we navigate through a rapidly changing world, integrating mindfulness into our everyday lives will not only help us to manage stress but also foster greater empathy and resilience. Undoubtedly, the evolution of mindfulness practices will continue to inspire and empower us, providing tools to cultivate a life filled with peace and purpose.

Emerging Research

As we look towards the future of mindfulness, emerging research is paving the way for a deeper and more comprehensive understanding of this ancient practice. In recent years, studies have begun to uncover the intricate ways in which mindfulness can positively impact our lives, shedding light on both its physiological and psychological benefits. The field of mindfulness research is expanding rapidly, with scientists and practitioners alike exploring its potential in various dimensions of health, well-being, and cognitive functioning.

One of the most fascinating areas of emerging research is the exploration of mindfulness' effects on brain structure and function. Through the use of advanced neuroimaging techniques, researchers have been able to observe changes in brain regions associated with emotion regulation, attention, and self-awareness among regular mindfulness practitioners. For instance, studies have shown that the amygdala, a region of the brain responsible for processing stress and fear, shrinks in size following consistent meditation practice. Conversely, the prefrontal cortex, which plays a key role in decision-making and executive functions, tends to thicken.

Beyond structural changes, researchers are also delving into the functional aspects of mindfulness practice. Functional MRI (fMRI) scans reveal that meditation can lead to increased activity in the default mode network (DMN), a network of brain regions associated with self-referential thinking and daydreaming. This increased activity in the DMN suggests a heightened state of self-awareness and introspection, which is a cornerstone of mindfulness practice.

Another promising area of research focuses on the immune system. Preliminary findings indicate that mindfulness meditation can enhance bodily immune function. Participants in mindfulness-based interventions have shown increased antibody production, suggesting a more robust response to infections. This opens exciting possibilities for using mindfulness as a complementary therapy for boosting immune health.

Mindfulness research doesn't stop at the individual level; its collective impacts on communities are also being studied. Schools, workplaces, and healthcare facilities are incorporating mindfulness programs to improve overall well-being. For instance, in educational settings, teachers have reported that students who participate in mindfulness activities exhibit better focus, reduced behavioral issues, and improved emotional regulation. In workplaces, mindfulness training has been linked to lower stress levels and enhanced productivity.

Moving into the realm of mental health, mindfulness is showing promising results as part of integrated treatment plans for various psychological disorders, including depression, anxiety, and PTSD. Mindfulness-Based

Cognitive Therapy (MBCT) and Mindfulness-Based Stress Reduction (MBSR) are two interventions that have gained significant traction and are backed by robust research. These programs combine traditional cognitive-behavioral approaches with mindfulness practices, resulting in more effective management of symptoms and improved quality of life for participants.

As technology plays an ever-growing role in our lives, its intersection with mindfulness is a dynamic field of study. Emerging research is increasingly focused on the efficacy of mindfulness apps and digital tools. While early findings are promising, indicating that technologically-mediated mindfulness can lead to reduced stress and improved well-being, this is a rapidly evolving field that requires further exploration to understand long-term outcomes and optimal practices.

Additionally, the emerging research is turning its focus toward specific populations and how mindfulness can be tailored to meet unique needs. For example, there's growing interest in how mindfulness can support aging populations. Studies are investigating its potential to alleviate symptoms of age-related cognitive decline and improve overall mental health in older adults. This may lead to mindfulness being integrated into standard elderly care practices, offering a non-invasive method to enhance quality of life.

Mindfulness and physical activity are also being explored in tandem. Researchers are studying how combining mindfulness practices with physical exercises like yoga, tai chi, and even running can amplify the benefits of both. Preliminary results suggest that such integrations can enhance stress reduction, increase emotional resilience, and improve physical health metrics like blood pressure and heart rate variability.

In the realm of clinical settings, mindfulness is being examined for its potential to aid in pain management. Chronic pain sufferers often face substantial physical and emotional burdens, and emerging research is showing that mindfulness can play a significant role in reducing pain perception and improving quality of life. Mindfulness-based pain management programs are designed to change the relationship individuals have with their pain, fostering a more accepting and less reactive approach.

Another key area of research focuses on mindfulness and its genetic implications. Though still in its early stages, scientists are investigating whether mindfulness practices can lead to epigenetic changes—modifications in gene expression that don't alter the DNA sequence but can influence how genes are turned on or off. This could have vast implications for understanding how a person's environment and practices can impact their health at a genetic level.

Moreover, there is growing interest in the impact of mindfulness on social relationships and community health. Mindfulness has been shown to enhance empathy, improve communication, and foster a sense of connectedness. Emerging research is exploring how these benefits can be harnessed to build more resilient and compassionate communities. This kind of research is crucial as it demonstrates that the benefits of mindfulness extend beyond the individual to society as a whole.

It's also worth noting the burgeoning field of mindfulness as part of integrative medicine. Practitioners are increasingly incorporating mindfulness into holistic health approaches that consider the mind, body, and spirit as interconnected. Research in this area seeks to understand how mindfulness can complement other treatments and enhance overall well-being.

As the field of mindfulness research continues to grow, it's essential to keep in mind that this is a journey of discovery. Each study opens the door to new questions and possibilities. The emerging findings are helping to demystify mindfulness and demonstrate its tangible benefits, making it more accessible and applicable to everyday life.

The future of mindfulness is bright, with new studies continually shedding light on its diverse applications and far-reaching benefits. Whether it's changing the brain, boosting the immune system, helping manage chronic pain, or fostering stronger social connections, mindfulness is proving to be a powerful tool for enhancing mental well-being. And with each new discovery, we're getting closer to fully understanding and harnessing the potential of this ancient practice in our modern world.

The Evolution of Practices

Mindfulness has come a long way from its roots in ancient traditions to becoming a vibrant part of modern society. We're no longer just sitting cross-legged in serene environments; mindfulness practices have evolved and diversified, catering to the frenetic pace of today's world. New methodologies continue to emerge, each designed to meet the evolving needs of a population seeking balance in an increasingly chaotic environment. The journey from past to present has been marked by adaptation, innovation, and a deepening understanding of human well-being.

Historically, mindfulness was closely tied to religious practices, primarily Buddhism. However, as it found its way into Western culture, it underwent significant transformation. The secularization of mindfulness, largely spearheaded by figures like Jon Kabat-Zinn, brought the practice into mainstream medicine and psychology. His Mindfulness-Based Stress Reduction (MBSR) program exemplified how ancient techniques could be reimagined to address modern health issues, making mindfulness accessible to a broader audience.

Today, we see an explosion of varied approaches. Digital advancements have played a key role in this evolution, offering tools that make mindfulness more accessible than ever. Mobile apps guide users through meditations, reminders encourage mindful moments throughout the day, and online communities provide a support network for practitioners. These innovations break down the barriers that once confined mindfulness to specific settings and allow it to seamlessly integrate into daily routines.

Moreover, the evolution of mindfulness practices has incorporated a wealth of interdisciplinary insights, drawing from psychology, neuroscience, and even sports science. Research has increasingly supported the efficacy of mindfulness, leading to tailored practices that address specific needs, whether it's for reducing anxiety, enhancing concentration, or improving emotional regulation. These evidence-based approaches enhance the credibility and effectiveness of mindfulness, making it a compelling option for a wider audience.

In recent years, we've witnessed a boom in niche mindfulness practices tailored to specific groups. From programs designed for corporate environments to mindfulness modules for educators and even specialized offerings for athletes, the flexibility of mindfulness practices ensures they remain relevant. This specialization is crucial, as it allows individuals to directly address their unique stressors and life circumstances, producing more meaningful results.

Mindfulness has also seeped into educational curriculums, with schools incorporating it into daily routines to help children develop emotional intelligence and focus. Kid-friendly techniques have been created, such as mindful breathing exercises, playful meditations, and simple visualizations, making it fun and engaging for younger minds. These early introductions aim to cultivate long-term well-being habits, laying the groundwork for a more resilient future generation.

Workplaces are another arena where mindfulness practices have evolved significantly. As businesses recognize the productivity and well-being benefits, they are integrating mindfulness programs into their corporate wellness initiatives. Techniques focusing on stress management, enhancing creativity, and improving interpersonal relationships are becoming common. These practices help create a more harmonious work environment, leading to a happier, more focused, and ultimately more efficient workforce.

Even in the realm of healthcare, mindfulness continues to prove its adaptability. Practices have been tailored to support patients dealing with chronic pain, insomnia, and even addiction. Medical professionals increasingly endorse mindfulness as a complementary approach, recognizing its potential to enhance traditional treatments. This validation from the medical community helps bridge the gap between ancient wisdom and contemporary medical science.

As we think about the future, it's essential to acknowledge the ongoing exploration and research in the field of mindfulness. The integration of virtual reality (VR) in mindfulness practices is a burgeoning frontier. VR can transport users to calming, immersive environments that enhance the meditative experience, offering a novel way to escape the bustle of everyday life. These technological advancements make mindfulness more engaging and accessible, especially for those who might struggle with more traditional methods.

Another exciting evolution is the inclusivity of mindfulness practices. Traditionally, these practices were often seen as part of a homogeneous culture, but today, there is a conscious effort to make mindfulness more inclusive. Practices and teachings are being adapted to respect and reflect the cultural backgrounds and personal experiences of a diverse global population. This effort is crucial for ensuring that mindfulness remains relevant and accessible to all, regardless of their cultural or social background.

The evolution of mindfulness practices isn't just about new techniques or technologies—it's also about a growing sense of community and shared experience. Mindfulness retreats, workshops, and group meditations have become more popular, fostering connections and shared progress among practitioners. These communal experiences can deepen individual practices, providing support and inspiration that sustains long-term commitment.

Furthermore, mindfulness is increasingly being seen through the lens of sustainability and social change. As practitioners become more present and aware of their actions, many find themselves more attuned to the broader impact of their lifestyles and choices. This growing awareness can drive more mindful consumption, ethical decision-making, and overall a more compassionate way of living that extends beyond personal well-being to include societal and environmental wellness.

Looking ahead, the future of mindfulness is likely to be characterized by continued innovation and integration across various sectors of life. We'll probably see further blending of traditional practices with modern sciences, leading to even more refined and effective methods. As new discoveries and technologies unfold, they will undoubtedly enrich the myriad ways we can engage with mindfulness, making it an ever-evolving path toward enhanced mental well-being.

In summary, the evolution of mindfulness practices mirrors our times— dynamic, adaptable, and intricately woven into the fabric of daily life. From ancient religious rituals to contemporary therapeutic interventions, mindfulness has proven its resilience and relevance. As we embrace its future, we cultivate a practice that not only navigates the complexities of modern existence but also connects us to deeper, timeless truths.

Conclusion

As we draw to a close, it's essential to reflect on the journey we've taken through these chapters. We've navigated the intricate landscape of mindfulness, from its historical roots to its modern-day applications. Along this path, we've discovered the profound benefits of meditation for both physical and mental well-being, explored various techniques to integrate mindfulness into our daily lives, and delved into the challenges and triumphs of building a sustainable practice.

At the core of this exploration lies a simple yet powerful truth: mindfulness is a gateway to a more peaceful, focused, and fulfilling life. It's about being present, fully engaged with whatever you're doing at the moment, whether you're savoring a meal, taking a walk, or simply breathing. This book has provided numerous ways to incorporate mindfulness into daily activities, encouraging you to see each moment as an opportunity to practice awareness.

For those who are just starting their meditation practice, remember that it's okay to begin with small steps. Setting up a conducive meditation space, choosing the right technique, and gradually extending your meditation time can lead to deeper, more enriching experiences. It's not about perfection but about finding what resonates with you and fostering a routine that feels natural and sustainable.

Diving into specific aspects like stress reduction, improving focus, and emotional regulation, we've emphasized the transformative power of consistent practice. The techniques outlined, from guided meditations to mindful walking, offer practical tools to help manage stressors, sharpen concentration, and respond more mindfully to emotional triggers. The benefits of these practices extend into every sphere of life, enhancing not only how we relate to ourselves but also how we engage with others.

Speaking of relationships, mindful communication and empathy are pivotal in nurturing connections. By approaching interactions with a sense of presence and openness, you can foster deeper understanding and compassion. This is particularly crucial in a world where distractions often pull us away from meaningful engagement.

Mindfulness and meditation also play a significant role in enhancing creativity and overcoming mental blocks. By quieting the mind and allowing yourself to be fully present, you can unlock new levels of creative potential and approach challenges with a fresh perspective. This book has offered insights into using mindfulness to inspire innovation and break through creative barriers.

The role of breath in meditation cannot be overstated. Techniques such as breath awareness and pranayama exercises are fundamental in anchoring your focus and calming the mind. These practices serve as a reminder that even in the midst of chaos, a few mindful breaths can restore a sense of calm and clarity.

Introducing children to mindfulness is a gift that can shape their emotional and cognitive development in profound ways. We've discussed simple techniques to help kids cultivate a practice of presence and awareness, and how building a family practice can strengthen bonds and create a supportive environment for mindfulness.

For those navigating the complexities of the workplace, integrating mindfulness into your professional life can reduce stress and enhance productivity. Techniques for mindful work habits and balancing work with mindfulness practices can transform your approach to both your career and personal growth.

During difficult times, mindfulness offers a beacon of resilience. Coping with crises, whether personal or global, becomes more manageable when we can ground ourselves in the present moment and approach challenges with a clear and compassionate mind. Building resilience through mindfulness equips us to face adversity with courage and equanimity.

Technology has both facilitated and complicated our mindfulness journey. While mindfulness apps provide accessible resources and guidance, a digital detox can also be beneficial in fostering deeper, uninterrupted practice. This book has offered tips for striking a balance between leveraging technology and disconnecting when needed.

Establishing a sustainable mindfulness practice requires setting realistic goals and tracking progress. By celebrating small victories and staying committed to your practice, you cultivate a lifelong journey of growth and self-discovery. The resources provided in the appendix offer additional support to continue this journey beyond the pages of this book.

Immersing ourselves in nature through outdoor meditation techniques and mindful nature walks further enriches our practice. Nature offers a unique and serene backdrop for mindfulness, helping us reconnect with the environment and with ourselves on a deeper level.

For many, the spiritual aspects of mindfulness add another layer of meaning to the practice. Exploring personal beliefs and integrating spiritual practices can deepen your connection to mindfulness. This holistic approach underscores the versatility and profound impact of mindfulness on every aspect of life.

We've also been inspired by the stories of transformation shared in these pages. Personal journeys and expert testimonies illustrate the transformative power of mindfulness and meditation, providing living proof of the positive changes these practices can bring about.

Throughout the book, we've highlighted the cultural variations and global perspectives on mindfulness, showing that while practices may differ, the underlying principles of presence and awareness are universal. This global outlook enriches our understanding and appreciation of mindfulness.

As we look to the future, emerging research continues to shed light on the science and benefits of mindfulness. The evolution of practices and innovations in the field promise to keep the journey of mindfulness dynamic and ever-relevant. Staying informed and open to new developments will ensure that our practice continues to grow and adapt over time.

In conclusion, mindfulness is not just a practice but a way of life. It invites us to live each moment fully, with intention and awareness. Whether you're just starting out or deepening your existing practice, the journey of mindfulness offers endless opportunities for growth, healing, and transformation. Embrace this journey with an open heart and mind, and may it lead you to a place of greater peace, clarity, and well-being.

May your path be filled with mindful moments and the wisdom to cherish each one.

Appendix A: Appendix

As we come to the end of this journey through mindfulness, let's take a moment to look at some additional resources and tools that can enrich your practice. This appendix is designed to provide you with a variety of options to continue exploring, learning, and growing in your mindfulness journey. Whether you're looking to deepen your understanding, find new techniques, or simply stay inspired, these resources are here to support you.

Resources for Further Reading

Diving deeper into literature can illuminate new facets of mindfulness and meditation. Here are some highly recommended books to consider:

- **"Wherever You Go, There You Are" by Jon Kabat-Zinn:** A comprehensive introduction to mindfulness and its practical applications.
- **"The Gifts of Imperfection" by Brené Brown:** While not solely about mindfulness, this book offers valuable insights into self-worth and vulnerability.
- **"Atomic Habits" by James Clear:** This book provides a great framework for habit formation, which can be applied to building a sustainable mindfulness practice.

Recommended Apps and Tools

Incorporating technology can streamline and enhance your mindfulness practice. Here are some apps and tools that have proven effective:

- **Headspace:** A user-friendly app with guided meditations for every occasion.
- **Calm:** Known for its sleep stories and breathing exercises, this app is perfect for evening relaxation.
- **Insight Timer:** Offers a large library of free meditations and talks from various teachers around the world.
- **10% Happier:** This app combines practical meditation techniques with evidence-based practices for mindfulness.

Mindfulness Retreats and Workshops

Mindfulness retreats and workshops offer a unique opportunity to deepen your mindfulness practice in a concentrated and immersive environment. Whether you're a beginner or an experienced practitioner, these retreats provide a space where you can disconnect from daily distractions and reconnect with your inner self. The setting, often in tranquil nature or serene spaces, helps to create an atmosphere conducive to mindfulness.

Attending a mindfulness retreat allows you to step back from the hustle and bustle of everyday life. These retreats often guide participants through various mindfulness practices, including meditation, mindful walking, and breathing exercises. Removing yourself from your usual environment can reveal the patterns and habits you might not notice during your day-to-day routine, offering fresh perspectives on your practice and life.

Workshops, on the other hand, can range from a few hours to an entire weekend. These shorter engagements are packed with practical information, interactive exercises, and group discussions. They are designed to introduce specific mindfulness techniques or deepen knowledge in certain aspects of mindfulness. The advantage of workshops is their accessibility; they're easier to fit into busy schedules compared to longer retreats.

Many retreats and workshops are led by experienced instructors who have dedicated years to their mindfulness practice. These teachers bring a wealth of knowledge and practical experience, helping participants navigate their individual journeys with compassion and wisdom. Their guidance can be especially valuable for tackling the common challenges that arise during meditation and mindfulness practices.

For those who find it challenging to maintain a regular practice, retreats and workshops offer much-needed motivation and structure. The shared experience of practicing mindfulness with a group creates a sense of community and accountability, reinforcing the importance of the practice. It's easier to stay committed when you're surrounded by like-minded individuals who share similar goals.

In addition to structured activities, retreats often provide ample downtime. This is a time to reflect, rest, and integrate what you've learned. Silence is often observed during these periods, encouraging introspection and helping participants focus inward. Taking a break from constant communication and social interaction can be transformative, bringing a much-needed break from the noise and chatter of daily life.

While retreats tend to be more intensive, offering a complete immersion into mindfulness, workshops are more flexible. They often focus on specific themes such as stress reduction, emotional regulation, or mindful communication. This allows participants to choose workshops that address their current needs and interests, providing targeted tools that they can immediately apply in their lives.

The settings for these retreats and workshops can vary widely. Some may be held in dedicated mindfulness centers, equipped with all the necessary facilities for comfortable and uninterrupted practice. Others may take place in remote locations, surrounded by nature, where the environment itself enhances the mindfulness experience. Forests, mountains, and coastal areas are popular choices, offering a natural backdrop that complements the practices.

Mindfulness retreats often incorporate a variety of activities that go beyond seated meditation. Activities such as mindful yoga, tai chi, and nature walks are commonly included. These practices help to embody mindfulness, bringing awareness to movement and the physical sensations of the body. Engaging in these activities can enhance your overall understanding and experience of mindfulness.

Another benefit of attending a mindfulness retreat or workshop is the potential for personal growth and transformation. The focused time spent on self-reflection and mindful practices can lead to significant insights. Many participants report experiencing a greater sense of clarity, purpose, and emotional balance after attending these events. This transformation often extends beyond the retreat, influencing their daily lives in positive ways.

For those new to mindfulness, workshops provide a gentle introduction. They typically cover the basics, offering a taste of different practices and techniques. Beginners can leave with a toolkit of mindfulness exercises they can continue at home. For the more experienced, retreats offer a chance to deepen and refine their practice, exploring advanced techniques and concepts.

The communal aspect of retreats and workshops shouldn't be overlooked. Sharing the experience with others creates bonds and connections that can last long after the event is over. Participants often leave with a support network of friends and fellow practitioners who can offer encouragement and advice as they continue their mindfulness journey.

In today's digital age, finding uninterrupted time to practice mindfulness can be challenging. Mindfulness retreats and workshops provide a time and space free from the distractions of technology. Many retreats even encourage or mandate a digital detox, asking participants to leave behind their devices. This can be a liberating experience, allowing you to fully engage with the present moment without the constant pull of screens and notifications.

Finally, the memories and experiences gained from these retreats and workshops often serve as a lasting source of inspiration. Participants can draw on these experiences long after the event has ended, recalling the peace and insights gained during their time away. These memories become a reservoir of calm and inspiration that they can tap into whenever they need.

Whether you're seeking to kickstart your mindfulness practice or looking to deepen an existing one, attending a mindfulness retreat or workshop can be a transformative experience. They offer a unique blend of guidance, community, and immersive practice that can significantly enhance your mindfulness journey.

As we reach the end of this section, consider exploring the resources and opportunities available for mindfulness retreats and workshops. They represent not just an escape but a journey towards a more mindful, balanced, and fulfilling life.